THE **SURVIVIN**
MEMOIR SERIES

I AM
A WOLF
TONIGHT

THE **SURVIVING BADLY**
MEMOIR SERIES

I AM A WOLF TONIGHT

SURVIVING BADLY

Cancer Loss, Complex Grief
and Other ~~Sh*t~~ Stuff – A Memoir

**THELMA
AINSWORTH**

BROWN
DOG
BOOKS

Published under licence by Brown Dog Books and The Self-Publishing Partnership Ltd, 10b Greenway Farm, Bath Rd, Wick, nr. Bath BS30 5RL, UK

www.selfpublishingpartnership.co.uk

ISBN printed book: 978-1-83952-886-6
ISBN e-book: 978-1-83952-887-3

Cover design by Kevin Rylands
Internal design by Mac Style

Printed and bound in the UK

This book is printed on FSC® certified paper

MIX
Paper | Supporting responsible forestry
FSC® C013604

'Feel the fear
But do it anyway.'

Richard Ainsworth,
eight years old

This book is dedicated to my two bundles of joy:
Dominic and Richard Ainsworth. You will always be loved.

This book is also dedicated to Child Bereavement UK and
the fundraising page for donations raised on their behalf by
Dominic and Richard Ainsworth:

www.justgiving.com/page/thelma-ainsworth-1699520336148

And a special mention to Erin and the Loss Foundation –
This is me planting a seed. Thank you.

Contents

Prologue

When the doctor came back into the room her demeanour had changed. Her chattiness and good humour had been replaced with a loss of eye contact and a body language which now betrayed her discomfort. She was still friendly but as she talked her words became more rambling in nature: she was stalling. I should have known then, as Jonathan and I waited for her to get to the point that the news was not likely to be good. And yet, when she finally said the word 'cancer' I felt unable to breathe. Her words hung in the air of that sterile, white and impersonal hospital room. My mind was initially blank, struggling to catch up with what had been said. It was then followed by one question which went round and round in my head in an endless loop – is this really happening? *Is this really happening?* The doctor continued talking, attempting to walk the fine line between empathy and her duty to impart the important information we needed to know. I caught the words 'pancreatic cancer' before I turned to Jonathan. He already looked diminished: his frame noticeably smaller than it had been for a long time, his face more lined and looking so much older than his 58 years. He had a small smile on his face as he engaged in conversation with the doctor, a former colleague from his period as a trainee doctor.

It was as though he already knew.

As they continued the discussion, my head began to fill with fog and disbelief. When the wailing came it took me by surprise before I realised that it came from me – I was the one howling with pain. The doctor and Jonathan stopped abruptly and looked at me. The doctor began speaking to me with what looked like genuine compassion, but I could not hear her. As Jonathan stroked my back I continued crying. I could not believe what I was hearing.

The doctor left to give us space. I looked up to face Jonathan, clutching his shirt. The enormity of what she said had begun to sink in gradually. This was no minor illness; we would not be leaving today with a prescription and a course of treatment for Jonathan to get better. The outcome was far worse than I had anticipated, far worse than I had ever imagined at that point: Jonathan had cancer. *Cancer.*

'Don't leave me, don't leave me.' I said the words over and over again to Jonathan. Although he had no choice in the matter, my tone was accusatory nevertheless. *Don't leave me, please don't go.* The fear that this would be the ultimate outcome began to seep through me. In the background I could hear Jonathan talking to me, exhibiting a patience that was not always present when we were alone. I could hear him saying that he would need to talk to me later, that he may only have three months to live. I could not absorb what he was saying. *This can't be happening. This can't be happening.*

In the taxi ride back home, I was in a daze. As we sat there holding each other, a rare occurrence in our marriage, Jonathan turned to me.

'I'm so glad that I met you, otherwise I would have been so lonely.' I had never heard him say those words before. I could see the tears in his eyes as he continued. 'I'm sorry.'

His apology surprised me. 'Why? What are you sorry for?'

'In all my relationships I never thought that I needed intimacy – never. I didn't realise how important intimacy was. But I realise now that I was wrong – intimacy is important. I was wrong. I'm sorry.' I said nothing and hugged him closer not quite knowing how to respond. Jonathan's honesty demonstrated a side to him I had barely seen throughout our marriage. It was bittersweet: feeling both appropriate and alien at the same time. We were silent for the remainder of the journey. When we got home we talked late into the night about the children and what would come next. It was a deeply traumatic night. In one fell swoop the whole landscape, the whole world had changed.

My world had changed.

Forever.

CHAPTER 1

The Courtship

*B*y the time Jonathan and I met I was already well into my thirties. Like a lot of women that age I was becoming anxious about my prospects of getting married and having children. Time was ticking, peers of my age group had already settled down, started the baby-making journey and I was still yet to get off the starting blocks. I was 33 years old when I decided to start dating with more vigour and energy than I could muster before. In those days, online dating was in its infancy, a mere toddler in the dating world, only managing the smallest of baby steps. By contrast, it was the lonely hearts columns that reigned supreme at the time that I met Jonathan and it was after answering my hastily written but efficient ad in the *Guardian* newspaper that I soon met him. The local bar in the bustling high street of Angel Islington was a fitting place for us to meet. It was vibrant and trendy, traits which I think Jonathan aspired to be even though he was already in his forties by then. When I first met him he was quirky, unassuming and different. Of the men I dated I had not found Jonathan to be the most romantic. He was however, one of the most straightforward in many respects, even though he could be deeply frustrating at times. Unsurprisingly our courtship was imperfect: he was not the chivalrous suitor. Nonetheless, we still gravitated towards each other as time went on.

On paper, we should not really have got on: he was a white, grammar school educated doctor from a typical middle class background dating a black professional, a lawyer and an officer in the RAF, but one coming from a considerably poorer background, a second generation Nigerian immigrant. However, somehow, at that time, we worked, notwithstanding our different backgrounds, and notwithstanding the 14 year age difference. And of course, we shared a love of running which became our main way of bonding.

Even so, there were occasions when it was clear that we were not always entirely suited: the debates/arguments we had and the lack of shared faith (I was a Christian and Jonathan was not) would often highlight the differences between us. As a consequence, we often fell out with each other, especially during those heated arguments when Jonathan would cast himself in the role of the intellectual scientist prepared to be provocative in his arguments as he attempted to disprove the existence of God to me. The constant butting of heads meant that we became enmeshed in what seemed like an endless on/off relationship loop before the gravitational pull between us became too strong to resist and we became a committed couple two years after we first met. And yet, throughout the turbulence that was present whilst we were dating, we also recognised in each other our common bond – which was that we were both stubborn in different ways, always differentiating ourselves from the crowd and often operating according to our own standards and ethics. In other words, we were both very distinct individuals who did not always conform with societal norms – we were special in that way and that kept us attracted to each other even as the disagreements raged. So, following each breakup, I found myself willing to give things another chance. And after each separation, when we came back together, we did so with more understanding of the other person and more humility which deepened our relationship. So, we continued dating. But I grew restless, wanting to settle down and start a family. Eventually Jonathan proposed, I think because he realised I would not wait around forever – and on that he was right.

There were real low points in the remainder of our courtship whilst we were engaged which should have been an enormous red flag and given us both reason to pause or at least question that strong pull to stay together. For instance, there was the time that I found out, quite by accident, that Jonathan had been seeing his ex-girlfriend whilst I had been based at RAF Lossiemouth in Scotland, my first posting as an RAF officer. I discovered he had been helping her financially and giving her the impression, at least initially, that he was still interested in her. Our relationship deteriorated and after he had returned from a trip to Brussels to visit a friend, we had an argument that made me realise that I was deeply unhappy. I packed my things and moved out of Jonathan's house – grateful at that point for the accommodation provided to RAF officers in the officers' mess. I felt deeply betrayed by Jonathan. Although our relationship had not been the stuff of dreams I thought that we were building something together for the future. I was distraught as I unpacked my belongings in the new room assigned to me at the mess. I felt like a fool. I also felt very, very embarrassed. I had told everyone about the engagement – my colleagues, my peers, my friends – feeling proud of myself that I too would be joining the growing band of married women that were beginning to dominate my workplace.

I couldn't bear to tell anyone.

It was my mother who persuaded me to give Jonathan another chance, telling me that he was a 'good man' and preying on my fears that I might end up alone with no spouse in the wings. But in truth I did not require a huge amount of persuading: I was realistic – I was in my thirties, in a job that would be extremely difficult for me to meet a suitable person; the prospects of having a child and settling down were diminishing with each birthday that approached. Perhaps this was not perfect but maybe with time and with work it would become a good relationship – at least that was what I hoped.

And so I stayed.

However, other than the constant effort needed in order for us to get along well in our relationship – there was also one other complication – the one area of Jonathan's life that became a huge element of our marriage and which I did not anticipate at the time: his family.

ও   ও   ও

When I first met Jonathan and he spoke to me about his parents it was with hesitancy. Even after we became an item he was reluctant about introducing me to his parents at first. When he did open up about his parents, he was, I think, very honest in his assessment. He said, 'My parents are the type that often put their own needs above that of anyone else. And my mother, well, she can be very controlling. Very controlling.'

I had been dating Jonathan for several months at that stage. I had found him at times to be critical of those around him. I had also found him to be a bit paranoid about the intention of others – sometimes making a negative assumption about another person which I did not always agree with. So I confess that I did not entirely believe him when he said this about his mother. In fact, I remember thinking that she could not be that bad or significantly worse than most mothers, including my own! This view did not change when I eventually did meet his parents.

I was slightly nervous on that day but I relaxed when I came into the living room and saw them both for the first time. Jonathan was seated on his favourite couch, strumming his guitar as he was prone to do at any given opportunity whenever in our living room. Patricia and Vincent were both seated on the remaining chairs in the room. Although both in their eighties they looked fit and mobile – looking well dressed and calm. Patricia was wearing a smart suit which looked expensive and tasteful. Her hair looked expertly coiffured and her jewellery showed years of experience in accessorising. Vincent was older but still had a striking head of hair. He walked with a stick but was able to manoeuvre around quite effectively without much assistance. His suit looked worn but fitting given his no nonsense manner. After the initial pleasantries he got straight to the point:

'So why on earth did you join the Air Force?!' His voice was not very loud but it dominated the room, filling it with his thick northern accent. Jonathan remained silent. I felt a bit taken aback – I had not expected to answer such a blunt question. In any case my answer clearly did not satisfy him. He asked another before getting onto the subject of wars and how he had managed to avoid being drafted to fight during the Second World War. Patricia also asked me questions, about my legal background, my job and so on. I fielded their questions but I began to feel under some pressure. Vincent was completely perplexed by my profession at the time – struggling to understand why a woman like me had joined the armed forces. I complied in answering his questions as politely as I could with as much good humour as I could muster but afterwards I thought the whole episode was a little bit absurd. I came away feeling as though I had just been interviewed for a job – and one which I did not feel I had been particularly successful.

However, despite the uncomfortable first meeting, I thought that my future in-laws were nice enough. They certainly seemed happy to meet me and after the interrogation they left to continue their evening at the show or gallery exhibition they had booked for their stay. But very slowly, over time, that initial assessment of them began to change.

Before we became a couple, Jonathan had had an arrangement with his parents whereby they would come and stay with him in London whenever they were coming to see a London show – either at the Royal Opera House or the theatre or whichever venue took their fancy. They normally did this in between their many and regular trips abroad on holiday, clearly determined to enjoy their retirement in full. This arrangement continued after we started dating and did not change, not even after I had formally moved in with Jonathan before our engagement.

I began to feel uncomfortable with the frequent visits to our house.

It seemed as though, without taking into account our schedule, Patricia would book the dates that she and Vincent wanted to come and they would then arrive and stay. And of course we would need to host them whilst they were here, notwithstanding our own plans or our workload or anything else that might impact on our ability to accommodate other people in our house. Now if Jonathan had still been single and lived on his own this would not have been an issue – but this was no longer the case. He was now engaged and living with his fiancée. And it was an issue for me.

It also seemed that every six weeks or so, we would be 'summoned' and have to make a journey in the car to visit Vincent and Patricia in their charming house in the Cotswolds. Now of course, they were elderly and were not as mobile as Jonathan and I. And of course those visits were often pleasant enough.

But even so.

Those journeys started to become onerous. I could never help the impression that I was deemed to be some sort of curiosity, an oddity to be examined – whether because I was so different to them in so many ways or for other reasons that I could not comprehend at the time. In any case, I struggled with those visits and soon began to resent their demands on our time.

So what Jonathan had said about his parents – about them putting their own needs and wants above those of others at times began to play out gradually. This came to a head on one of our visits to see them. By then they had been coming to London quite regularly and this routine had now become well established.

We had arrived at their house earlier that day. We had not eaten dinner yet and were in the living room having pre-dinner drinks. Vincent broke the silence by saying they had something important that they wanted to talk to us about. They then proceeded to lay out the 'problem'. I remember Vincent taking charge:

'We wanted to talk to you about something. It's to do with our visits to come and see you. The parking space in front of Jonathan's house can only take *two* spaces.'

Vincent had a way of speaking that made him emphasise those words that he deemed important to enable him to make the point that he wanted to make. The important word in this instance was clearly the word 'two'. He continued:

'But between us we have three cars...'.

Vincent paused. It took me a while before I realised he had no intention of continuing. He had presented the problem and it now hung in the air like an unpleasant odour. There was silence after he had spoken. Jonathan looked mildly exasperated but said nothing. Patricia was silent too but joined her husband in looking at me and Jonathan expectantly. This was clearly our problem to solve – not theirs. I was confused because I saw no 'problem'. As far as I was concerned these visits were being made primarily for their convenience – to experience the delights of London but without any of the costs associated with a short-term stay in the capital. Jonathan and I however worked and both of us needed our cars. For me the solution was obvious:

'You can both park on the street. I have visitors' parking vouchers – as long as you park on the street within a white parking bay you will be fine.'

This was clearly not the response they were expecting.

It was I that should move my car and allow them to park their cars closer to the house. It was I that should make way, *not them.* They never actually said this of course, but it was implied in the very long silence which followed after I spoke.

A very, very long silence.

Eventually Jonathan broke the log jam:

'It's fine – I'll move my car and park it on the street.'

A solution which worked for them but with an outcome that they clearly had not expected. At the time I did not understand why Jonathan had sacrificed his own convenience but it was clear that deferring to his parents was what he was used to – and something which they expected me to do as well. This expectation reared its head again when it came to my wedding.

Years before we had gotten married and our kids were born, Jonathan and I had gone on holiday to Toulouse. One day we were visiting an old town near there. As we explored a nearby church, we had a discussion about marriage. Jonathan had teased me about the fact that if I was lucky, then when we married we could do so in St Paul's Cathedral – because his mother had an OBE courtesy of the strides she had made whilst working in academia. It had not been clear at that stage whether we were headed for marriage. So although the prospect of getting married in a cathedral had excited me at the time – it also felt more like a fantasy that was highly unlikely to come true. However, when we eventually got engaged and I started the task of making the wedding arrangements, any thrill I felt about organising a wedding at this famous London landmark soon became marred once those arrangements began to involve my in-laws.

It was early 2011 and I was now based at RAF Northolt, the home of the Service Prosecuting Authority. I was one of a number of officers within the legal branch of the RAF and also within the Prosecuting Authority itself, dealing with prosecutions and preparing cases for court martial. It soon became apparent that I would struggle to do all the work required with the wedding planning as well keep up with the demands of my career. I hired a wedding planner to assist me and felt immense relief after I had done so. The wedding arrangements then became much more manageable – and even more enjoyable. But it soon became clear that Patricia expected to be kept abreast of all the details concerning the wedding. The few occasions when we had seen them during our engagement there had been some questions about the wedding arrangements which I believe I had duly answered.

In retrospect there must have been a great deal of frustration bubbling beneath the surface at my crisp and efficient answers.

So it should not have come as a surprise that a month or so before the actual wedding she invited Jonathan and I to come and stay with her and Vincent for a couple of nights over a weekend. I did not come on that occasion, choosing instead to stay at home and do some work. Jonathan attended without me and it would appear was bombarded with questions about the wedding arrangements – to most of which he had no answer of course! Well, no matter, for shortly after that visit I received an email from my mother-in-law asking the questions that she needed to know. She began the email with pleasantries expressing mild disappointment that I had not been able to come and stay for a visit with them and noting that Jonathan seemed happy and relaxed, 'if a little vague about the wedding arrangements.' Then she delved in and set out the 'few questions' she had about the wedding. Those 'few questions' ended up being no less than 11 questions ranging from 'how many guests?' and 'what music will there be?', all the way to 'who will be giving speeches?' and 'when and where will the photos be taken?'.

My initial instinct was to answer a couple of questions and then to say that she would need to turn up on the day and find out the answers herself – like everyone else would! However, in the end I did reply with a fuller response – with more patience than I was feeling – and referred Patricia to my wedding planner if she had any other queries. This turned out to be not quite enough. At the wedding, Patricia and Vincent were cold and standoffish to me. After Jonathan and I had exchanged vows and were signing the register with them, they barely looked at me. The only assumption I could make for their reaction was that I clearly had not indulged their every whim by answering their multiple questions to the nth degree. It was a cold atmosphere with them but I carried on with my wedding day, largely enjoying it despite everything. Jonathan and I felt so close and in sync on that day – and I wanted to relish that feeling for as long as I could – so I focused on him and me, thereby relegating everything else to a background white noise. At the end of the day, after the reception and whilst we were on the steps of St Paul's Cathedral, having the last photographs taken, it was then that my mother-in-law really made me furious. My wedding planner and I had organised a wedding car to take Jonathan and I back to our house after the reception had ended. The other guests going back to our house including Patricia, Vincent, my brother-in-law Tom and his family, were to take their own taxis back to the house. This was not good enough for Patricia however. As I was preparing to enter the wedding taxi with Jonathan, my mother-in-law planted herself in front of me:

'What happens now then?'

'We will all go back to the house. Kathleen, our wedding planner, will call you a taxi so you and Vincent can head back.'

Silence. Clear disgruntlement on her part. I turned away – not completely oblivious but at the same time focused on the rest of the wedding day and not on trying to pacify my mother-in-law. Jonathan then intervened. He took me aside. Our wedding car, with the beautiful white satin ribbon across the front of it was quietly waiting for us. Patricia and Vincent had clearly seen the car. Jonathan turned me so that I faced him and said quietly, 'You better let her ride with us otherwise she will bitch.'

My natural instinct was to say 'no' and ordinarily I would have done. Without hesitation. However, I had literally just got married to Jonathan, and clearly this was going to be an issue. I look back on that day even now and wished fervently that I had stood my ground. But I can hardly be blamed for deferring to my new husband. So I relented. And therefore on the way back to my house, in what should have been a special moment between my husband and I in our wedding car, that moment was shared with two others: a pair of octogenarians, grinning from ear to ear as we travelled through the City of London back to our home. This would not be the last time my in-laws would frustrate me. There would be more to come in the future.

But for now, when we tied the knot on that sunny day in March 2011, in St Paul's Cathedral, in the OBE chapel, I believe that Jonathan and I were happy – at least it seemed like it. For our honeymoon, we trekked the Annapurna trail in Nepal with its stunning scenery and the holiday became a great bonding adventure. We were both fit from our running and the trekking for 10 hours a day was a wonderful once in a lifetime experience. Although Jonathan became ill with mountain sickness and we had to cut short the trekking, we remained in Nepal, relaxing in the south of the country which was beautiful, with air that was still pure and unpolluted. We felt very lucky to be there – it was a truly memorable time. I wish we could have stayed that happy.

CHAPTER 2

The Husband

My marriage to Jonathan was difficult.

I am aware of course that every marriage has its ups and downs. I am aware that there are many couples that put on the facade of a perfect partnership in public which quickly descends into an acrimonious atmosphere at home. My marriage was not the worst marriage in the world (I hope) but at times it was not always good.

We were happy to be married to each other at first. For a long time I felt settled. I was part of a unit, a partnership and I felt this could be the beginning of a positive chapter in both of our lives. But as our marriage continued, it soon became clear that it would not be smooth sailing. The differences in our personalities started to shine through. Jonathan was more cerebral and intellectual. He loved the mental gymnastics of a debate and being contrary for the sake of it. I was more emotional in my thinking, more prone to attachments and more tribalistic in my loyalties. There were many periods when we got along and were able to do things together particularly well as a family with the children. However, there were more periods when we were very distant from each other. And as the marriage traversed such rocky plains as childbirth and child-rearing, my mental health issues following the birth of my children, money issues and much more, I craved more than anything someone who truly loved me and saw me and accepted me as I was. Jonathan did say that he loved me, sometimes, but I often struggled to believe him when he did. There was very little in the way of natural affection between us. There was no romance between us. Oh, there were 'romantic' trips away – but always organised by me. There were no huge romantic gestures on my birthday from Jonathan. Valentine's day became quietly ignored with each year that went by. I yearned for Jonathan to do those things for me, but he never did. I remember the odd bunch of flowers once in a long while – but almost always this was preceded by an argument. From my point of view, I regressed into myself during the course of my marriage. I became incredibly capable at dealing with things on my own. Yes, we worked as a team, especially when we were on holiday and needed to, but for the most part I felt and was alone even as I dealt with and sometimes overcame challenging situations. And I had plenty of those in my years of marriage to Jonathan.

The last few years for me before Jonathan's diagnosis had been torrid. In the spring of 2016, I gave birth to my youngest child, Richard. This wonderful, sweet, cute little boy was a bundle of joy when he finally arrived but my pregnancy with him and the subsequent birth had been extremely difficult and traumatic. I had been in labour for days, had to be induced and then had to have an emergency C-section. All a far cry from the positive and uplifting tales of childbirth shared by members of my NCT cohort. It was also not too dissimilar from the trauma of the birth of my first son Dominic, who had needed an emergency ventouse delivery after the passing of meconium whilst still in my womb. I had hoped with Richard for an easier birth more in line with the rather improbable NCT seamless water birth delivery they showed us at the end of our group sessions. This was not to be, however. Instead, my C-section with Richard had led to complications including a spinal fluid leak requiring further surgery to deal with it. In the end, after all the medical interventions, my hearing had been impacted, and I had lost a lot of blood (I would later learn as I was put on iron tablets that there had been a serious discussion between the medical professionals about my needing a blood transfusion). I felt absolutely dreadful in the days after giving birth. Poor Richard had also been born premature and needed to spend a few days in the neonatal clinic, all of which added to the stress of the situation. I am not ashamed to say that by the time I arrived home with my newborn baby, mentally and physically I felt completely overwhelmed. Following his birth, I was eventually diagnosed with PTSD and, with some reluctance, started taking antidepressants for the postnatal depression that had enveloped me. I soldiered on during maternity leave looking after my children, deeply grateful for the space I had from the frenetic pace of work to be able to stay at home and just breathe – as I got used to having a newborn in the house as well as Dominic, who was then a lively three-year-old boy with boundless energy. I was eventually medically discharged from the RAF ending my 10-year stint there as an officer in the legal branch. Slowly but surely, I gradually came off the antidepressants and began to recover. I began to feel better about myself and life in general. Conversely however, I was not feeling that way about Jonathan and our marriage.

The lack of spontaneous affection and external demonstration of love from Jonathan became increasingly intolerable for me in our marriage with each year that passed. Jonathan's aloofness and distance – something which I had of course been aware of and had accepted during the early part of our relationship when I was independent and able to take care of my own needs, was suddenly a huge problem during those times when I was at my most vulnerable: during fertility treatments and with it the various miscarriages I had when we had issues conceiving, when I was pregnant, during the traumatic births of my two sons, the aftermath of those births, the difficulties of being a new mother and so on. His lack of understanding and tenderness at those moments became more and more difficult to endure. I remember being heavily pregnant with Dominic, walking with Jonathan to an NCT meeting in Ealing, which took us via an uphill street. I was not quite waddling, but my gait was certainly affected as we made our way to the venue. Jonathan could be a very fast walker when he wanted to be and although I was pregnant he would not wait for me, often striding off into the distance before then waiting for me up ahead, hands behind his back. How I hated it when he did that. I felt as though I were an afterthought – looking after me in that instance and putting me, in my pregnant state first did not come naturally to Jonathan. After minutes of trying to catch up with him I was reduced to tears. I asked him to wait for me and to make the point I forced him to slow down by putting my arm through his. Jonathan complied but he was not overly enthused by this intervention. This made me feel more neglected and isolated. Or there was the occasion a few weeks later when we were at the NCT meeting (one of the last ones before the course ended), the lady running the proceedings asked everyone to talk about who did the meal cooking in their household. All the other couples – the males in particular said lovely positive things about their partner whether they were great cooks or not. Not Jonathan: his assessment that I was not much of a cook and to make a joke out of it, may have been accurate but it upset me greatly. This was not surprising given the setting, my vulnerability and increased sensitivity at the time.

In common with a lot of women who are about to give birth or who have recently given birth, I always felt much more vulnerable and tender during those periods. So I probably expected more from Jonathan in terms of understanding and care at those times. I recall voicing this to him a few times, certainly enough for him to understand how I felt on occasion. I hoped that it would prompt him to change. When that was not forthcoming, it deepened my disillusionment with my marriage. So much so that very soon after the birth of my eldest in 2012, after being so upset and frustrated with Jonathan, I contacted a law firm and spoke with a solicitor with a view to starting divorce proceedings. I was so distraught and angry at the time. I was also completely depleted and did not feel that I had the energy to carry on with him whilst also being a new mother. That was a particularly low point for me and our marriage, a mere 18 months after we had exchanged our wedding vows. I did not go through with it but for a moment the prospect of being free of a marriage lacking in affection was as liberating as it was traumatic.

It was not just the lack of external affection which made me unhappy. Sometimes Jonathan would not always treat me very well, not often but enough for it to really hurt when he did. I am not saying that I am perfect in every way. I have my own faults like everyone else. I am sure that if Jonathan were still here he would have his own version of events and the role that he felt I had played in our relationship. However, there were times when Jonathan could be a bit … unpleasant. I remember saying the same to him a few times, particularly after a long argument, often declaring that he could be 'deeply unpleasant' when he wanted to be – he did not disagree with me. One occasion that comes to mind was at the wedding of one of his friends. We had gone together as husband and wife.

At the time we had had our eldest son; our youngest son was yet to be born. Being Jonathan's friend I was the outsider so I did not know everyone there. A guest, someone that Jonathan knew, came over to us and started speaking to Jonathan. I was with Jonathan at the time and watched as the two were engaged in conversation. Jonathan ignored me and carried on speaking to this person. He did not introduce me or try to include me in what they were talking about. Eventually I drifted away. Later in the evening when I recalled that segment of the night, Jonathan admitted that he had excluded me deliberately. He wanted to see what I would do and had 'respect' for me when I walked away. The significance of what he had done and the casual way in which he had done it did not sink in at the time. Yes I felt deeply hurt that evening but the fact that he had deliberately set out to exclude me and make me uncomfortable and unhappy did not fully resonate until maybe weeks afterwards. And when it did it became another brick in the wall between us in our marriage, a wall that was growing bigger and stronger with each month and year that went by.

And just as I had done at his friend's wedding, walking away from Jonathan became something I began to think about more and more. The arguments we had as our marriage progressed got worse and worse. With each fight we revisited the tensions of the past and so even the most minor disagreements became so difficult to work through and resolve effectively. For my part, I did not feel able to cast Jonathan in the role of a supporting partner with whom I could navigate life's travails any longer – instead, at best, Jonathan was a neutral body who was there in the background fulfilling a parental role alongside me but not *with* me; and at worst he was a person who caused me unhappiness and grief on an increasingly consistent basis. My trust in Jonathan and in our marriage was disassembling and the emotional see-saw I was on within our marriage went into freefall. By then any conflict became dangerous, a potential spark that threatened to burn down the whole fabric of our marriage. And the spark could be on almost any issue. One day there was a parking problem on our street. When Jonathan came home he was furious with me. He asked me why I had not re-parked his car. I had been busy with the children and other errands all day – it had not even occurred to me to do that. I became upset with him because I perceived it as one in a long line of micro-aggressions against me and did not think he was being fair at all. I was so upset I went upstairs crying and shaking. I needed to get away. With tears streaming down my face, I hastily packed an overnight bag. I told him I was going away for the evening and would be back tomorrow. I could see the surprise on his face but also a stubbornness – he had no intention of apologising. I went outside and stood in front of the door. I realised that on the face of it, this was an intense overreaction but on the other hand I felt emotionally raw – I did not feel that I had the energy to be picked on yet again. I had no idea where I was going – I had no plan. Whilst stood outside in the cold, I eventually called a nearby hotel and managed to book a room for the night. I then called an Uber cab and went there, relieved to get away even for only a short period.

The problems in our marriage, as all-consuming as they were, did not involve just me and Jonathan however. My in-laws were ever present in the background, weaving a complex web of intervention into our daily lives.

Despite Jonathan and I being married, the constant visits from Patricia and Vincent which had been present during our courtship, continued. In fact, if anything, those visits became more frequent. Although we were now busy newlyweds with our own lives and careers, their visits to London culminating in a stay at our house carried on uninterrupted. I began to find their intrusion into our lives suffocating. One of the best examples of this was a year after we got married – on our wedding anniversary.

On our first wedding anniversary I had anticipated that we would spend that time together alone, Jonathan and I. But it was not to be. Patricia had organised a trip to London – a visit to the theatre and dinner the exact weekend of our anniversary. I remember seething with resentment at the time but I did not have the courage to explicitly tell them 'no'. Instead, on what should have been a romantic day to be spent with my husband, I found myself seated next to Jonathan at a dinner table in an elegant restaurant in London – with Patricia and Vincent opposite us. Patricia gleefully pointed out at one stage that 'today is your wedding anniversary'. I replied curtly, 'yes it is' and I had rather hoped that she would get the message – but she did not. She clearly thought that it was appropriate for her to take ringside seats at the first wedding anniversary of her son and his new wife. In much the same way that she had thought it was appropriate to ride in our wedding car, it had not occurred to her that visiting us the same weekend of our anniversary, would be crossing some sort of boundary. I felt annoyed with myself for allowing it to happen but Jonathan was present too – the whole incident did not seem to bother him in the slightest. It seemed that as our marriage progressed and as the incursions by Patricia and Vincent increased, Jonathan's resistance waned whilst mine became turbocharged. I resented having someone in my life dictating to me or imposing on me without my having any discernible control over it.

The birth of our children highlighted the amount of control that Jonathan's parents had in our lives and it began to grate on me, particularly when I was at my most vulnerable. After the trauma of Dominic's ventouse birth, I was tired, overwhelmed and emotional. By the time I finally reached home I was in a sombre mood. Jonathan's ability to fully understand how I was feeling and to offer unconditional support was limited. As usual. In this scenario my in-laws wanted to visit immediately after I had given birth. They called Jonathan shortly after we had arrived and from his part of the conversation I could hear Patricia already making plans to come and Jonathan of course acquiescing – without any reference to me. I shouted out, 'No, they can't come!' I had just given birth and was too vulnerable to cope with a visit from them. Jonathan then came with the phone and handed it to me so I could speak to Patricia. I took the phone from him and proceeded to have an argument with her. She was insisting that she come down immediately and I tried to explain to her that this was not a good time. We must have discussed the generic topic of her visits to us. All I remember was what came next. With Jonathan standing outside the door eavesdropping, I ended up shouting down the phone at her, 'Would you please just give us some space?!!!' That phone call presented a turning point in our relationship. The result was that Jonathan and I managed to get some breathing space: although the visits to London continued – this no longer involved a stay at our house. I was relieved.

Patricia's control over Jonathan did, however, continue. A few years later I was pregnant with my second child, Richard. I had been going to NCT classes in the lead up to the birth and the penultimate class was on a Saturday. Jonathan had accompanied me to the previous classes. However, on this particular Saturday, Patricia had arranged for one of her visits where we would all have to go and see her. Jonathan, the ever-obliging son had already agreed to this. I told Jonathan that we could not go because we had an NCT class to attend.

My husband refused to come to the class.

'We can't go. My mother is expecting us.'

'But we can go and visit any time. This is one of the last NCT sessions. I'm too heavily pregnant to go on my own – I need you there!'

'We will just have to miss it this week.'

We continued to argue. Jonathan would not be moved – even though I was in the third trimester of my pregnancy and was begging him to come. I realised that there was only one thing I could do. When Jonathan went upstairs to grab his things, I called Patricia. I told her that we had an NCT class which I needed to attend and Jonathan was refusing to go – insisting instead that we still go to visit her – despite the fact that there was no special reason or occasion for the visit. Patricia appeared to find the whole thing amusing. She agreed to talk to Jonathan. We ended up going to the NCT class after all. And as I sat in the class with my husband by my side I could barely believe that his presence was only possible courtesy of his mother's permission. It was a dire state of affairs.

At times it felt like a large portion of the years of my marriage to Jonathan meant being treated like an appendage to Patricia and Vincent's lives. The six-weekly summons continued after our marriage: Patricia would inform Jonathan that she would like him to visit and he would then jump to attention – which meant we all had to troop down to Oxfordshire like obedient children. Each visit would entail packing up our car for the days' visit and travelling there to see them. And after we had our sons, inevitably the heavy lifting of child duty would always fall on my shoulders – it was I that would pack for the boys and for myself, coordinate bedtime routines and their meals. It was exhausting and yet I did this and more. Jonathan, on the other hand, would almost revert to being a child in his parents' company. He would take great pains to spend time with them and accommodate them in ways that I did not feel he did with me. Oh how I resented it. I felt at times like a nobody – nothing more than a glorified nanny – there to look after the kids and thereby enabling everyone else to enjoy themselves.

My resentment sometimes played out in churlish behaviour on my part and I acted in ways which were unbecoming, childish and unkind. For instance, during one of our many visits to their home, Patricia and Vincent informed us about the dinner that they were hosting at the famous Le Manoir aux Quat'Saisons for all the family to celebrate their wedding anniversary. Vincent looked pointedly at me when he said, 'Everyone must attend!'. No doubt that comment was influenced by the fact that at that stage I had taken to not always attending their invitations to come and visit them. And this had clearly not gone unnoticed. Hence the instruction from Vincent that I toe the line.

I did not like the prospect of this at all.

And so from the moment that Vincent uttered those words I decided that I would not attend – important family occasion or not. When they confirmed the dates of the dinner in an email I responded to express 'regret' that I could not attend but I was very busy with work. I added that Jonathan would be attending and I was sure that they would all have a lovely time. I could not contain my glee at swerving the doomed family function along with the satisfaction of not doing what they wanted – I was seizing my autonomy and I was thrilled. In the battle of wills however, there is no greater opponent than my in-laws. They wanted me there and it would appear that they would stop at nothing for that to happen. So, incredulously, the date of this dinner was changed – it was moved to another weekend and the invitation was sent out again with Jonathan informing me of the new date.

'I can't make it.'

Jonathan's eyes widened and then narrowed. He knew of course what I was playing at.

'Thelma, you have to go. My mother will be upset.'

I played it innocent. 'I'm afraid that I can't make it. My sister's birthday is that weekend – I can't do it.' I had not actually planned anything for my sister's birthday at the time and truthfully, any birthday celebration could have been postponed if necessary – but they were not to know that.

Jonathan looked wary. 'You tell her – I'm staying out of this.' With pleasure, I thought. I took time drafting the email to Patricia, telling her in the most apologetic manner that I could not make the anniversary dinner. Again. However, they were not to change the date because of me as Jonathan would be there (of course he would) and I was sure that they would all have a good time. I am not proud of the delight I took in knowing that I was throwing a fly into the careful ointment that they had created. But I was annoyed and exasperated with them. And with the amount of control they had sought to wield over me through Jonathan, and I felt that I needed to fight back.

It felt good.

I felt sated and thought that was the end of the matter. Not so. I was wrong.

At work a few days later I took an anxious call from Jonathan. 'You have to come to the anniversary dinner!' Jonathan rarely panicked but his voice sounded strained. Even so I rolled my eyes as I continued my work on the screen. This was all becoming a little bit irritating. 'Jonathan I told you I can't make that date. You're still going. What's the big deal if I don't make it?' I could sense Jonathan beginning to lose his temper. 'My father has just been on the phone shouting at me. My mother received your email and she is crying. They think you don't like them and they really want the whole family there at this do!' Well, I thought, she certainly gets points for being astute. And for winning the fight: I knew the game was up. I had had a good run but on this issue, as on so many similar issues, Patricia and Vincent's wishes would prevail. Again.

Jonathan's deference to his parents was there all the time. It was present even in the most absurd way. In 2018, a year before he died, Jonathan had decided to knock down an internal wall in our living room thereby creating a larger living space. This resulted in the need to redecorate the whole living area – a task which I assumed as a couple we would be perfectly able to manage ourselves. Again I was wrong.

'Why is your mother coming with us to pick out a rug?'

'Because I invited her.' We were in the new living room that afternoon, with the children outside playing in the garden. We had decided to inspect the new space and take stock of what needed to be done which would include new rugs for the recently varnished wooden floor. Then Jonathan casually dropped the bombshell: his mother would be coming with us on our shopping expedition.

'But surely this is something we can do or I can do as the woman of the house. Your mother should not be coming!'

'I want her to come. She has a good eye and good taste and I value her opinion.'

I was seething but felt impotent – he had already invited her and he was not going to change his mind. So, we all traipsed around John Lewis looking at curtains and rugs, Jonathan and I and our two children. And his mother. The humiliation of having my elderly mother-in-law accompanying me and my husband on a shopping trip for items in *our* home was bad enough. What made things so excruciating was that Jonathan saw absolutely no issue with this. The fact that this upset me made no difference to his actions.

That feeling of being overlooked by my own husband was a constant theme in our marriage. It made me feel powerless. It made me feel bitter. And it continued for the remainder of our time together, serving as a backdrop to our relationship. It was especially poignant on special occasions and holidays that would require spending excessive time with my in-laws. Like Christmas time.

Every Christmas we would go to stay with his mother and father for a few days and with each year I found it increasingly difficult. I would do the usual round of buying presents for everyone, including Jonathan's family – his parents and his brother's family. However, this would not be good enough for Jonathan. He would insist on going out by himself to Westfield, the bustling shopping mall a few miles away, just before we were due to leave and visit them, in order to buy *more* gifts for his family – making a real effort for them. He bought not only gifts for his mother and father, but also for his brother Tom, his sister-in-law and their children. He would then take the time and effort to wrap those presents for them.

Now most married couples would not duplicate that kind of effort but this just demonstrated how separate we were from each other: there was me and then there was Jonathan and his family. In his mind, he still needed or wanted to go out and buy these gifts again.

The worst thing about all this was not so much the fact that Jonathan would go out of his way to buy these additional gifts for them – it was the kind of spontaneous effort he made for them – tapping into his instincts about what would make a great present, something he rarely, if ever, did for me.

During the last Christmas holiday we spent there, in 2018, Jonathan had gone out in his customary fashion to buy gifts for his family. Except this year he bought June, Tom's wife, some really lovely gifts: a beautiful jewellery box and a feminine wicker basket bag. These kind of gifts I would never have received from him. Jonathan's gifts to me were laboured: either bought after asking me what I wanted or more likely, when I was not forthcoming with a list, he would present me with gifts of a more practical nature. These gifts this year to June hurt me a lot. It showed that he was capable of romantic feminine gifts – he had just not wanted to make the effort *for me*.

It was also deeply frustrating because despite the effort that Jonathan made to go out and buy these individual gifts for his brother, his sister-in-law and his nephews and niece, it was not clear to me that that amount of effort expended by Jonathan was reciprocated at all. I have no doubt that his brother and his sister-in-law were oblivious to the huge efforts he made.

I did not want any part of it.

When my brother in law and his family eventually arrived at his mother's house for the Boxing Day dinner, I stayed upstairs in the room I shared with Jonathan for a long while.

I did not want to come down and face them. In retrospect it was unfair for me to resent Tom and June – after all they had not asked for Jonathan to behave in this way towards me; my real anger should have been reserved solely for Jonathan. However, unfair or not, I felt hurt and disrespected that day.

And that became entrenched in me: the lack of respect and consideration I felt from Jonathan I also felt in some ways from Jonathan's family. It was a constant feeling I felt throughout the time I was married to Jonathan – always bubbling under the surface even on those occasions when it appeared that we, as in I, Jonathan and his family, were all getting on very well. I felt completely invisible at times: my sole job was to look after the kids and facilitate things so that the important people – which included Jonathan somewhere in that hierarchy – could enjoy themselves. There were subtle ways that this was demonstrated, such as during those visits to my in-laws. However, there were also occasions when my position (or lack of) within the family was more than apparent. It was several months before his diagnosis, that Jonathan was called by Patricia one afternoon when we were out in the park with the boys. We were in a park that we did not go to often but it was spacious and largely deserted, with swings and slides which the children played on whilst Jonathan and I sat and watched. Jonathan answered on the fourth ring and moved away slightly to take the call but I could still hear the gist of the phone call and it soon became clear that it was Patricia on the other end and she was asking him to come and visit. Again. Except that this time it came with a twist. When he finished talking to her, he came back and confirmed what I thought I had heard. I was furious.

'What do you mean she wants you to look after Vincent?' I tried to keep my voice low so the boys could not hear.

Jonathan did one of his exaggerated sighs. He always did this when he thought I was being unreasonable.

'She and June want to come to London to visit and my mother wants me to look after Vincent.' I could just about understand why Vincent needed help. Over the years Vincent had become less mobile and independent – and could not be left unattended for long periods of time. But still …

'Why can't Tom do it?'

'He's busy.' This was most likely true. Although Tom was a consultant like Jonathan, he tended to do a lot of private practice work which often crept into the weekend. This was in contrast to Jonathan who was committed entirely to the NHS and to his clinical practice as a consultant in HIV and infectious diseases at the north London hospital he had worked at for many years. And also it would seem, to putting his mother's needs above mine.

The whole situation completely riled me.

'What about me and the kids? What about our plans for the weekend?'

Indeed, what of our plans. My mother-in-law was coming all the way here to London with her other daughter-in-law to visit and see in the sights. She was going to casually borrow my husband to look after her own husband when she could easily hire a carer. This meant I would be left to look after my kids on my own at the weekend, with no help from Jonathan. And this was not forgetting the lack of respect towards me: even though I actually *lived* in London and was also her 'daughter-in-law', there was no suggestion of inviting me along to this 'girlie day out in the City'. Of course, all this was lost on Jonathan – he was happy to oblige his mother – with no reference to me or my feelings.

The bitterness in me grew. There is no doubt that over the years, the feeling of being an outsider, of being invisible, of being ignored in relation to Jonathan's family became more and more overwhelming. It was important during those times to cling on to those periods when we could play at being happy – even if we weren't – such as during holiday times.

Our time as a family was definitely at its best when we were all on holiday together. Each summer since the children were born was marked with a week or two basking in the warm sunshine in the South of France. During those times, for the most part, we functioned quite well as a family. Jonathan and I would be more relaxed and it was very hard not to feel more content and even happy when you are in one of the most beautiful regions in France. Jonathan was a loving father to our boys and the holidays were a great opportunity for him to demonstrate his paternal instincts. However, the balm of the yearly summer holiday was eventually not enough to soothe the growing cracks in our relationship. Our last holiday as a family in France was a couple of months before Jonathan was diagnosed with cancer. It also provided the setting for what would be the most acrimonious holiday we had ever had since the children were born. By now there was real tension between us. Although we were still sleeping in the same bedroom at home, whilst on holiday we seized the opportunity to sleep in different rooms in the charming spacious gite that we had rented, which was on secluded grounds with an indoor pool and balconies giving us a wonderful view of the countryside. With the boys sleeping on another floor and therefore completely oblivious we did not hesitate: the separate sleeping arrangements were a natural progression for us at that stage, being entirely consistent with the level of estrangement between us. I felt relief to have some space from him but also sadness at what we had become.

A few days after we arrived we decided to take a trip out to the local village. We always brought my car on holidays as it was the bigger vehicle. Before we headed out to the village Jonathan started to pack my car with the rubbish we had accumulated in the gite. When I protested as I was concerned that the rubbish would leak out into the car, Jonathan snapped at me. He said that I was the bane of his existence and something to the effect that I was the problem in the family. We got in the car and drove to the village. As soon as we got there, we went out for a walk with the kids. We reached a park and sat down to start to eat lunch. At that moment, my profound unhappiness came through. I felt trapped and burdened with Jonathan, who was turned away from me in stony silence. I did not want to be there. I quietly picked up my things and walked away. I went to a nearby cafe and sat there after ordering a soft drink and a snack. I felt deep sadness to be away from the children. But I could not deny the immense relief I also felt to be away from the conflict with Jonathan. I must have sat there for almost an hour, pondering my life and my marriage, willing myself to return but unable to move. I was beyond exhausted. I wondered how I could carry on and the impact that all this was having on the children. As I sat there, I saw them walking by, Jonathan holding Richard with Dominic walking jauntily and happily by his side. I wiped away my tears and rejoined them and being the good actors that we were, Jonathan and I carried on as though nothing had happened and went on to have a day of fun with the children.

When we got back to England, of course we carried on. We managed to get on with the daily function of family life but there was no denying that our marriage was in a very poor state. In the last few weeks before Jonathan was diagnosed with cancer we had our last explosive argument. We had been arguing in the morning during the school rush about something minor and inconsequential. Jonathan accused me of not doing something. I burst into tears and through tears tried to explain to him about my mental health issues and the mental fog and confusion that would descend on me from time to time, often stopping me from functioning effectively. I wanted and expected him to put his arms around me and hug me and be sympathetic and caring. Instead, I still remember his mocking tone as he said to me, 'Yes, there's always something.' It was really the tone that I found deeply upsetting: rude, contemptuous, unsympathetic. In moments like this it seemed that he cared very little for me.

'If you speak to me like that again, I will divorce you.' I spoke slowly and with conviction. Even through tears and anguish there was anger inside me.

'If you want a divorce Thelma, I will give you one.' He stared back at me, devoid of emotion. It was clear to me then that he had most likely been thinking about ending our marriage as much as I had been. It made me feel even more wretched than before. I don't believe that we ever really recovered from that argument. But despite our words, our threats, I don't believe that either of us had any real appetite to make the terminal break from each other.

That was the thing about Jonathan and I in our marriage: no matter how unhappy we both were we colluded with each other to keep things going – not quite willing to let go of the strong bonds that had held us together until now. For the children's sake mainly but also maybe for our own sake. What a scary prospect it is to start the process of separation with two young kids in tow. Better to cohabit, to keep a skeletal crew on board the marriage ship and keep it sailing for as long as possible. In doing so we lived largely separate lives, talking for short bursts during the day but mainly keeping ourselves to ourselves on a daily basis.

So the state of our marriage and its lack of warmth and care meant that I did not pay as much attention as I should have done when he lost weight and started complaining incessantly about his stomach pain. Indeed, there was no reason for me to suppose that Jonathan was seriously ill in the weeks leading up to his diagnosis in October 2019. He had lost weight yes, but he had also been running quite a bit which would have explained his leaner build. For as long as I had known him, running had played a huge part in his life. At one point in our courtship, he had referred to it as 'the love of his life'. And through cycles of his running, particularly when he was consistent with it, he could lose quite a bit of weight. At that time he had been pretty devoted to his daily fix. Even our holiday in the South of France at the end of August had not put in a dent in his determination: he ran every day whilst we were nestled in the French mountains, undeterred by the uphill routes that he would need to navigate and often running for up to six miles or more on most occasions. I also thought his leaner build could be due to stress, as he had been under a lot of pressure with work – particularly in his role as R&D director which he combined with his clinical practice at the hospital he worked at full time. He had also been working very hard in his spare time on his research project – a project that he had been working on for years linked to his clinical practice. He had put himself under a great deal of pressure to complete it by his own self-imposed deadline. All of this combined, I surmised, would have taken its toll on him mentally and physically. And, even as he complained about the persistent pain that had begun to plague him, he was still going to work every day – he rarely missed a day off work. So the truth is that there was absolutely no way I could have foreseen what was ahead. I was also more than a little distracted.

I had been feeling for the first time in many years some optimism about one area of my life: the possibility of a return to my career after leaving the RAF to stay at home and look after the children. Richard would soon be starting nursery and therefore be joining his elder brother by being in full time education. I had begun to think very carefully about what I wanted to do job wise. I became enthused by the prospect of a return to work and managed to make contact with an organisation that helped former City lawyers like me return to private practice. The chance to carve out an identity for myself again outside the realms of motherhood or being a wife gave me motivation and purpose. So by the time we had that last family summer holiday together in 2019, I was feeling quite positive about my future – at least in the area of work. The flurry of activity with CV preparation and back to work seminars kept me busy and my mind off Jonathan and our marriage. It was a distraction that I embraced and leaned into wholeheartedly. So when Jonathan became thinner I did not assume that it was anything sinister. But, as time went on, and especially in the latter weeks before his diagnosis, Jonathan did start referring more pointedly to his weight loss, sometimes looking at himself and commenting on how thin he was. However, such was the state of our marriage, and our estrangement, that when he did this I did not take him seriously. If anything, I remember being offended when he had talked about his weight loss – I had thought that it was an indirect dig at me because I had gained quite a lot of weight since the birth of our youngest son. I look back on that and feel immense guilt that I had not insisted that he check himself out with a doctor – even if his response would most likely have been 'I don't need to, I am a doctor!' as was always the case whenever I suggested he take medical advice.

I should have known it was serious when he came home early on Thursday 3 October 2019. He had done his bloods earlier in the week and that had concerned him enough for him to see his own GP the day before, on the Wednesday. The doctor had examined him and noted that his liver seemed a bit enlarged. She had referred him for some scans at the hospital. Even at that stage, following the few times that we discussed it and debated what it could mean, I did not perceive it to be anything very serious. Jonathan himself said very little but did not appear unduly worried and I took that as a sign that there was probably nothing too ominous about it all – it would likely be something and nothing. The following day, on this Thursday, we were meant to go to our weekly session of Relate relationship counselling. We had been undergoing Relate counselling for a while, at least 18 months by that stage. It had been my effort to try to do something about the state of our marriage. Jonathan had initially refused to go when I suggested it. I had told him that I was going to go ahead with it – without him if need be and if he did not attend then I would 'empty chair' him and make a decision about our marriage following the initial course of sessions. This prospect had clearly not sat very well with him and he had reluctantly agreed to come. And so we had gone, every other week on a Thursday.

Not this Thursday however.

Jonathan came back from work and went straight to bed. He marched up the stairs and threw himself on the covers. He did not leave the bed all evening. This meant we had to miss our counselling session. And it meant that I had to look after the kids all by myself. Again.

I couldn't help myself – I should have had sympathy for him but all I felt was resentment and annoyance that I was left to run the household whilst he stayed in bed having a rest! I thought he must have picked up a bug of some kind and would be better in the morning – he clearly did not have the energy to go to a session or anywhere else at that time. I left him in bed and spent the evening tending to the kids.

The next day, on the Friday, Jonathan went to work saying that he was going to repeat his bloods again. He came home at lunchtime.

'What's wrong? Why are you back so early?' I was slightly annoyed when Jonathan strode through the door. I had been sorting out some admin before starting the process of packing. I was going away that weekend to a hotel for a much needed break. There was no prospect of that now.

'I've had the results of the bloods back.' Jonathan paused. 'I don't like the look of them.'

I looked at him properly 'What do you mean?'

'The results are not right. I just don't like the look of them.' Jonathan sat down. He looked worried. This in turn made me worried too – because Jonathan rarely looked like he was out of his depth. He always had a confidence about things especially where it concerned medical issues. Every diagnosis of cold, flu and other minor infections that Jonathan made in our house was always done with an air of certainty and supreme knowledge. The fact that he had come home in the middle of the day, which he rarely ever did, made me realise that this was potentially serious. I focused on Jonathan.

'I think I need to go to hospital.' Those words from Jonathan confirmed that whatever was wrong with him was very serious indeed. Jonathan had a special aversion to attending hospitals in his spare time, especially as a patient. If he felt he needed to go, then it would have been for a very good reason.

'OK, let's get you to hospital then.' Whatever I felt for Jonathan, in that moment I knew I needed to be there for him.

We debated which hospital to go to. He was not keen on St Mary's Hospital because he may bump into former colleagues but it was the closest hospital and in his view the best equipped one. As I organised our transport there and sorted out the urgent childcare for our children, despite the apparent gravity of the situation, I still thought that however ill he was, he would recover soon enough.

How wrong I was.

CHAPTER 3

The Diagnosis

*A*s I look back on that afternoon now I wonder how much Jonathan knew. His years as a doctor, would have given him the experience to make a decent stab at what was afflicting him. On the other hand, I was completely oblivious. Having decided to focus on my career again, and feeling that I did not entirely want to waste my time at the hospital, I spent the first portion of our time there on my phone researching career coaches (even though I really could not afford it). Surprisingly enough, as much as I was disappointed that my plans for a well needed rest had been thrown into disarray, I did not resent Jonathan whilst we were in the hospital. If anything, it brought us closer – we were facing a difficult situation together and in doing so we reassembled the parent team that only made its appearance in front of the kids when we were on holiday together. Except this time we chose to do this voluntarily – for Jonathan's sake. After I had exhausted my search for very expensive and inaccessible career coaches, we sat in companionable silence for a lot of the time, sitting closely together as we observed the others in the hospital. Jonathan and I rarely spent much time together enjoying each other's company so the long hours we spent together at the hospital was unusual for us. We managed to chat and keep each other engaged, speculating on what could be wrong with him but avoiding any form of forensic examination – after all we would soon find out and

I was convinced that whatever it was would be serious but treatable. At one point we even talked for a while about the TV show *Chernobyl* which we had both watched (separately of course). With its plot centred on the cancer victims who had become ill following their exposure to radiation, I see now that it was like a prophetic intervention, a little hint, a whisper of the role that this illness would soon play in our lives.

There is nothing more dispiriting than sitting in a hospital waiting room for hours, trying to fill the time and space foisted upon you whilst keeping a lid on your anxiety. The longer we waited the more keenly we felt the imbalance of power: it was the hospital which had complete control of our time, keeping us there on hold at their will until it was our turn at the top of the queue. By contrast our options were limited – we could stay and receive help, whenever that might be or leave and give up our place. We stayed. There was no choice. The hospital waiting room was busy, with nearly all seats taken; the clinical smell of antiseptic winning out against the odour of all the different people populating the corridor and the room. The experience of waiting in a hospital together was not new to me and Jonathan. The last time we had gone to hospital and had sat and waited had been because of our eldest son. He had had lumps in his neck, swollen lymph nodes which had been there for quite a long time but which had grown sufficiently to make us worried. We had come to St Mary's Hospital then, watched as he had his bloods taken and had then gone for a walk in Hyde Park whilst we waited for the results of those blood tests to come through. It was one of those rare occasions where we had both been waiting on the medical results with bated breath. We were now doing the same.

As the night wore on and it became evident that we would not be back until much later, I arranged for another nanny to take the boys for the night as a sleepover. I thought about how worried the boys would be and how I would explain our absence but almost in the same instant I put it to one side. We would be back soon enough, Jonathan would be fine and we could resume our lives as normal – the boys would not be any the wiser.

After we had been waiting for at least a few hours we finally had some good luck: Jonathan bumped into a consultant colleague from his past – the very thing that he had hoped to avoid but which turned out to be quite fortuitous in the end. She ended up looking after Jonathan and managed to take him in for a scan after looking at the blood results that he had brought in. We eventually got brought into a room to wait. By this time it was pretty late. I decided to go out and buy us some food and returned with Kentucky Fried chicken which we ate in the room. Even at that stage, Jonathan's appetite was not what it was and he left a large portion of his food untouched. The door opened shortly afterwards and the doctor came back in: the moment of truth had arrived.

 & & &

As we collected our things from the hospital room to make our way home, I felt like I was floating. I wondered idly if I would wake up soon even as I helped Jonathan down the stairs to the hospital exit and to the taxi rank. I was relieved when we finally reached home – as though the normal familiar surroundings could somehow erase the past several hours. But of course, it could not. The first night we spent together at home following the diagnosis was awful – a living nightmare where the complete shock and despair that had enveloped us at the hospital now hung in the air of our bedroom. Everything seemed the same, the same bed, the same wardrobe, the same clutter – and yet everything was so very different. I was a different person. Jonathan was a different person. We were simultaneously in the same reality but also living in another one. One which would involve hospital visits, chemotherapy, prognosis and ultimately death, or at the very least constantly living in its shadow. This was not the way that our lives were supposed to be. Whether we had stayed together in our marriage or not, either scenario had always featured both of us being alive and healthy, navigating life and parenthood alongside each other if not together. The death or permanent absence of one of us had never been contemplated. This actual reality was jarring and terrifying.

  ⁝ ⁝ ⁝

The next morning when I woke, for a moment, one blessed moment, I forgot everything and felt anxious to start the day as usual.

And then I remembered.

Like a crushing weight on my chest I lay immobilised on the bed. Jonathan was still sleeping and as I watched him I wondered if he would experience the same upon waking – forgetting and then remembering.

The hospital.

The cancer.

I felt new tears pricking my eyes. But my pillow was still damp from all the tears I had shed last night. It now felt uncomfortable. I shook myself and got out of bed.

Today was the birthday party of Peter, one of Dominic's friends. In the end it was a godsend. It provided a legitimate reason for the boys to be out of the house and to give Jonathan and I some much needed space. At this stage, the prospect of telling the children filled me with dread. It was something that I absolutely could not contemplate doing at that time. Jonathan and I never explicitly discussed it – we were still in a state of shock. Even if we did, there was no way that either of us were ready to tell our children who were so blissfully unaware, that their lives had been turned upside down and to watch them enter the world of fear and despair now inhabiting my life and Jonathan's life. There would be time for this soon enough. Just not today. Not now.

I had arranged with Valerie, our nanny, that she would take the boys to the birthday party after picking them up from their sleepover. We would also need her to look after the boys a lot that weekend as Jonathan and I absorbed the shock of his diagnosis and went to tell his parents. We made the decision to tell Valerie everything in that case. Valerie had been such an integral part of our lives at that point – like another member of the family in many ways after all her years of looking after the boys since Dominic was one year old. We told her in the kitchen, with me feeling tearful and Jonathan being characteristically matter of fact and calm. It seemed unreal saying it out loud to a third person but there it was: Jonathan had cancer. At the moment it was being treated as pancreatic cancer but more tests would be needed to confirm that. And the ultimate prognosis.

Valerie was shocked and upset but stoic too. We swore her to secrecy – we needed time to digest the news and to tell family members first before announcing it to the world. Valerie nodded – in complete agreement with us. Then promptly told

Kathy, Peter's mother, at the birthday party who reached out to me shortly thereafter. I forgave Valerie. In hindsight, it may have been unfair to impose a burden of that magnitude on someone. The need to share and make sense of such a seismic event would have been overwhelming. In any case, we very much needed her. Jonathan had made the difficult call to his brother Tom, and told him about his diagnosis. We then decided to visit Jonathan's parents the next day without the children and tell them the bad news in person. Valerie had agreed to look after the boys whilst we did that. Tom and his wife June would inform Vincent and Patricia that we were coming and would be waiting with them when we arrived.

Later that day, whilst the boys were still at the party, Jonathan became restless. He wanted to go for a walk – just me and him. He said he needed to clear his head. There was no question that in that moment Jonathan really needed me – maybe to reflect and try and make sense of this madness. I probably should have felt good about him turning to me and I certainly wanted to do the right thing by him. But in all honesty it also felt strange to be constantly by his side in this way, as his confidant and companion, particularly given our respective positions just a few days ago – like trying on a new outfit that I had always wanted but once it was on being undecided as to whether it really suited me after all. I felt confused. I felt conflicted. But I also realised that I had a huge responsibility at that moment towards Jonathan and our family, and one that I would not and could not shirk at any cost.

We drove down to Hampstead Heath, one of his favourite places to run. We parked the car and walked a short distance through one of the quieter areas of the park. It was very rare for Jonathan and I to go to Hampstead Heath by ourselves

just for a walk. In the days before we had children we would
often run in the Heath together. We would start off at the
same time but with Jonathan being more impatient and also
being a short distance runner he would go faster, then run
off and double back to find me whilst I plodded on at my
slower more predictable pace. An hour later, I would still be
going but Jonathan would have run out of steam and spend
the remainder of the time valiantly trying to keep up with
me as I finished my circuit. As we picked our way through
the clearing and found a bench I felt sad as I remembered
our past runs in this park. We would probably never run
together again.

We sat in silence for a while, holding hands. This part of
the Heath we were in felt familiar – I was sure that I had been
here before. It was a large grassy area, not quite deserted but
spacious enough to afford us privacy from the other walkers
dotted about. The trees ahead were dense, almost dark as it
led into the forest area of the park. Jonathan loved the Heath.
He always claimed that he knew it 'like the back of his hand'
because of the many times he had gone there. I felt Jonathan
shudder and I turned to him – he was crying.

'I really wanted to finish my research project. I don't
want to go!' I held him close against me and stroked his
hair. Jonathan's research project had always been of such
importance to him. It was not surprising that he would think
of it now. I made soothing noises and let him sob, crying
silently with him. Since the diagnosis this was the first time
that Jonathan had cried, had actually shown fear of what was
to come. In fact I had never seen him cry like this in all the
time I knew him – with such abandon. I realised then that
Jonathan had never really showed me his vulnerability at all –
not like this. I cupped his face in his hands and told him 'Your

research legacy will live on Jonathan. But your greatest legacy will always be Dominic and Richard.'

It was almost dark before we left the park. As we walked back we held each other and felt closer to each other than we had done in so long. We did not know it then but that would be the last time we would ever go to the Heath together again. The next day, with Valerie again looking after the boys, I drove Jonathan to see his parents and relay the news. As I did, I ruminated on the history of my relationship with my in-laws. Even though my relationship with them was not always warm, I did not expect the reception that I received when Jonathan and I arrived at his parents' house.

CHAPTER 4

The Deterioration

*A*s we approached his parents' house, Jonathan shifted uncomfortably in his seat: he was not accustomed to being driven. It was normally I that would be in the passenger seat with Jonathan driving us up to the gravel path of the house – a typical storybook style building common in the Cotswolds. The surrounding front garden was as immaculate as ever: Jonathan's parents took great pride in their garden. We got out of the car and went in through the open front door. As agreed, Tom and June were waiting with Vincent and Patricia when we arrived. In comparison to his older brother, Tom looked vigorous and healthy, exhibiting his sturdier build with confidence. June waited quietly by her husband's side, very slim with shoulder-length brown hair and little make up. After greeting them, Jonathan went straight into the living room with Tom to tell his parents. As I crossed the threshold my wariness escalated – I was no longer in my home, in my comfort zone – I was amongst Jonathan's people. I went into the kitchen. Even at that stage I felt like an intruder: the urge to retreat and give them space was overwhelming. Whilst Patricia and the men were in the living room June came into the kitchen to join me.

'He looks awful!'

Upon hearing June's voice I turned to face her. I nodded but said nothing. Although it was said in a manner conveying concern, I felt at that point that I was under attack in some way. I interpreted her statement as '*He looks awful. How could you not notice? Have you not been looking after him?*' A single statement – but one heavy with blame. Or perhaps it was just my guilt and she was merely giving voice to my own internal criticism.

As if to prove the point, what followed were further questions from June which again on the outside could be construed as concerned probing questions given the gravity of the situation and her medical background as a nurse, but in retrospect I felt that they were almost accusatory. I answered as best as I could, giving an up-to-date account of all that had happened but I felt at all times uncomfortable.

Shortly afterwards, Patricia came into the kitchen. She put some food in the oven, the tray shaking as she tried to manoeuvre it onto the oven shelf: she looked devastated. I sensed in equal measure her shock at being told about Jonathan's cancer and her annoyance with me. She avoided looking at me – there were no hugs or attempts to console – just a distance and silence.

My discomfort grew.

We had the lunch as planned. We gathered at the table in the dining room, picking at the food laid on by Patricia. Jonathan at this stage was visibly ill and weak – he looked pale and tired with his shrunken frame making his clothes seem several sizes too big for him. Seeing him through his family's eyes I suddenly felt so guilty. Was June right? How could I not notice what Jonathan had become? *How had I missed this?* Jonathan must have been in some pain but did not say so explicitly. He managed to sit at the table for no more than 10 minutes before it was too much for him. He excused himself, waving away my offer to help him, and went upstairs to rest, holding himself delicately as he navigated the stairs.

I stayed at the table, feeling some obligation to remain, especially as Jonathan had indicated he did not need me in that instant. I soon wished I hadn't. With Jonathan gone, the discussion at the table turned in earnest towards treatments and oncologists and I spoke to them candidly about the diagnosis and all that had happened. There was only a muted response from them all. Tom listened to me, avoiding direct eye contact, his animosity towards me coming in waves. I had no idea why this was the case. I had not fallen out with him explicitly. I could not recall any conversation between us that could be construed as a disagreement. Nonetheless, I was clearly not liked, not wanted. When the discussion turned to next steps concerning medical treatment and intervention Tom said that he had spoken to a good oncologist. There needed to be further testing before treatment because the doctors were not entirely sure that the cancer had originated from the pancreas. I remember expressing impatience with all the delay:

'Why don't they just start the chemotherapy and once they know what type of cancer it is they can make it more targeted?'

'They have to know what type of cancer it is – if they start chemotherapy blind it can cause more harm than good.' Tom answered firmly whilst still avoiding my gaze – he did not want to look at me.

'Would it speed it up if Jonathan goes private?' I asked, willing to consider all possibilities regardless of the cost.

Patricia chipped in at this point, 'Whatever needs to be done, should be done – money is no object!'

Tom's response was that we needed to go through the appropriate channels for now. Although oncology was not his area, his contacts in his profession were useful enough to give him the information that he, and we, all needed to know. Tom made clear that there may be a time when the private medical route could be considered but it was too early for that now.

I eventually went upstairs to join Jonathan. The discussion had thinned out and I was feeling tired. I felt disconnected from them and very alone. I sensed that with my back turned I too would be the focus of a discussion – and not in a positive way. Jonathan was lying on one of the two single beds that occupied the spare room whilst I sat on the other. We spoke very little – Jonathan was exhausted and struggled to keep his end of the conversation so I let him rest. He lay on the bed and closed his eyes. I watched him a while, taking solace in the fact he was still breathing. He was still here. *Still here.* After about half an hour, Tom knocked on the door and came into the room. He spoke to Jonathan briefly, updating him on the oncologist that he was going to make contact with. He then said goodbye to him, shaking his hand. He turned and started walking towards the door. I moved to say goodbye to him but he ignored me entirely, brushing past me as though I weren't there. So I had not imagined the animosity. The only thing that I could not understand at the time was why? What had I done? Whatever the reason I soon found out one important thing: this was just the beginning.

ಜ ಜ ಜ

Once back in London, it seemed like everything moved in a slow haze. I was living in the moment but at the same time quite detached. It was as though someone else had taken over my body. With Jonathan's diagnosis the whole world essentially turned on its head. He promptly got signed off sick by his GP and was then home full time. As for me, all the plans that I had regarding my career were thrown off course. My return to work schedule was slowly dismantled as I absentmindedly cancelled chats and reminders for meetings with job coaches, noting that one meeting would have clashed with an oncologist hospital appointment that I was due to attend with Jonathan. There would be no clash now – for I had a new job in addition to being a mother: I was now also Jonathan's full-time carer and he and all his medical appointments and treatments would take priority now.

Pervading everything during that period, especially shrouding my actions was one emotion that I struggled with: guilt.

'I feel like I am partially to blame for his cancer. I helped to cause it.' I was tearful but resolute. I believed what I was saying. I was at home, sitting at the kitchen table. The boys were either at school or at nursery and Jonathan was upstairs resting in our bedroom. I was alone speaking to Phillip, my psychiatrist. I had been assigned a six-week session with the RAF mental health unit following my discharge from the armed forces. This was further treatment for the PTSD that had been diagnosed whilst I had been serving and which had been caused by the traumatic birth of Richard all those years ago. I had just reached the end of my sessions when Jonathan was diagnosed with cancer. This would be my last phone call with Phillip before my therapy would officially end. I had just told him what had happened.

'Why do you say that? How are you to blame?' His voice as always was calm and soothing. I would miss my sessions with him.

'We were going through a difficult period and we argued a lot.'

'I don't think that that would be enough to cause cancer in someone.' He said this gently but firmly. I was not convinced.

'I am not saying that I am fully to blame but I am partially to blame – a portion of the blame can be attributed to me and the stress of our marriage.' I felt tears well up again. It sounded absurd as I said this out loud but at the same time I knew deep down that it was true. It had to be – it was the only thing that made sense. Phillip was silent for a while. Then he asked quietly:

'How much would you attribute to it?'

'I would say about 20 per cent.' I believed this implicitly and despite Phillip's efforts to steer me away from this line of thinking, I would not be moved. I felt partially responsible for his illness and it would take a very long time before I began to believe otherwise. In the interim, this innate guilt stayed with me, constantly overriding many other emotions that I felt at the time.

In many ways the guilt was useful, often acting as a propeller for my actions whenever I felt inertia or tiredness begin to take over. There were so many things that needed to be done during the period following Jonathan's diagnosis – practical things, sensible things, which I clearly did do. However, it was done in the style of someone wading through treacle. It was very much like having an out of body experience when you see yourself doing things but you do not feel them as you do it.

One major thing that needed to be dealt with after his diagnosis was the matter of the Relate marriage counselling that we were undergoing. A few days after we had returned to London following our visit to his parents, I sent an email to our counsellor informing her of Jonathan's diagnosis, that we were now concentrating on fighting the cancer and getting him better and confirming that we would no longer require her services. The glowing picture I gave of Jonathan and I going into the sunset with all our marriage woes effectively 'melted away' was not quite the truth. I think though that I very much wanted to believe it. At least that is how I thought it should be. There was certainly some reconciliation – but for the most part things were still not perfect between us. But this did not matter – I was committed entirely to my family. My whole world became incredibly narrow and focused solely on the boys and on Jonathan. One of the hardest things during that period was telling the boys about Jonathan's cancer diagnosis. Jonathan had become so visibly ill and weak at that point it could no longer be avoided. It was unspoken between us but we both knew that I would have to tell the boys and to do so on my own. Not just because Jonathan was too weak but also because in matters like this, we rarely ever acted as a united front – in childcare matters the burden always fell on my shoulders. On this issue however, I did not complain. To assist me, I bought some books on cancer with a particular emphasis on explaining cancer to children. Richard was just three years old at the time and far too young to try and engage with effectively at that point. Dominic on the other hand was six years old and unfortunately was old enough. I do not remember specifically how or when I did it – but I did. I have a vague recollection of telling my eldest son and fielding lots of questions. I remember trying to be upbeat about it and perhaps I gave the impression that with proper care and medicine his father would be well again. I suppose it had to be painted that way because how else could a six-year-old boy deal with the fact that his father had been diagnosed with an awful illness and might die? He needed hope and I didn't feel that I had much option but to give it to him at the time. Even so, almost overnight, I saw Dominic change, his maturity morphing into the persona of a child haunted by anxiety and trauma. I felt guilt again – I had caused this new disruption to our family and at times like that I did not wish to carry on.

But with the guilt and the fear pushing me, I did carry on. I had to – there was at the time no one else and if I fell then like a pack of cards everything else would fall too. So on I went. And there was so much more to do. In such a short space of time there was a flurry of medical appointments, all of which I had to coordinate and organise in between dealing with the children and ensuring that their life carried on as normal. Apart from seeing the consultant in the hospital, Jonathan also had to attend hospital on different occasions for a liver biopsy and a PET scan for a number of reasons but one of which was to help determine the type of cancer he had. The day of his liver biopsy was one of the most stressful and insane days that I experienced after Jonathan became a cancer patient. In my determination to carry on life as normal as possible, I had taken Jonathan to the hospital for the liver biopsy, then picked up Richard from nursery for a playdate which I did not stay for because Valerie came to take over looking after him. I then shot off to the school to watch Dominic perform in the school concert for violinists, before rushing back to the hospital to rejoin Jonathan. It was mad. It was crazy. But I did it and did so without question – this was now my new normal.

As time went on Jonathan regressed more and more into himself. His once curious and inquisitive nature had been silenced by the cancer that was spreading inside him. Whereupon once he would have been researching his illness for hours trying to pinpoint exactly what type of cancer he had, from where it had originated, and how far it had spread – now his response was indifference. I am not sure that he knew that his time was imminent, what I am sure of was that he had begun to take on the aura of a man who had given up the fight. As a highly skilled and experienced doctor he probably knew on some level that the outcome would not be positive. And yet on other occasions he clung to hope. He mooted with me on a number of occasions about the type of cancer it was. He expressed his hope that it may be leukaemia. That would be the best worst case option. Leukaemia or blood cancers can be more treatable and the prognosis can be more optimistic. However, as time wore on that optimism faded and soon there was no more talk of what kind of cancer it could be. Whilst I scoured Google and online medical articles about cancers and tried to determine what kind of cancer it could be from his symptoms, he turned in on himself: he effectively switched off. He became consumed with a desire to finish reading a book that he had bought from Westfield. In fact, that trip to Westfield in order for him to buy a book was one of the first things that we had done following his diagnosis – me driving us to Westfield and watching as Jonathan spent hours browsing the bookstore before making his selection. Of course he never managed to complete reading that book – Jonathan's time was more limited than either of us could ever have imagined.

Although we knew that he had an aggressive form of cancer, his deterioration happened so quickly once he had been diagnosed that it still took us by surprise. He became weaker and weaker – becoming increasingly housebound, then floor bound, room bound and then bed bound. During that time I wish I could say that relations between us were good or at least easier because we were bonded by the common enemy of cancer. Unfortunately this was not true. Jonathan was still Jonathan. And I was still me. He had his moments of vulnerability but ultimately his frustration and no doubt fear at his illness made him bad-tempered at times. About a week after his diagnosis I called a TV repair man to fix the TV we had. Whilst Jonathan and I were having lunch in The Island pub the TV repair man called to reschedule. Jonathan became cross when I told him how much it would cost to repair the TV and said that he would repair the TV himself. When I gently tried to point out that it would be more sensible to get this repair man to do it, Jonathan became very annoyed and rude. I was in tears by the end of the lunch. When we got back to the house, true to his word, Jonathan did attempt to try and fix the TV but he could not do it. He was incredibly weak at that point. It was no surprise that he eventually had to give up and then went upstairs to his room to rest. I was left to quietly reassemble all the TV paraphernalia and tidy up before going to collect the boys.

With each day that went by I begun to feel increasingly strung out from looking after Jonathan as he rapidly declined while still looking after the boys and trying to give them a semblance of normality. On a typical day I would drop the boys off at school, look after Jonathan in the day and try repeatedly to make contact with the Macmillan nurse who was supposed to help (I could never reach her). I would then try to coax Jonathan into eating something for lunch (his appetite was fading). Then later I would go to pick up the children – Dominic from school and Richard from nursery. I would try to keep up the boys' extracurricular activities and then make dinner for the boys and also try to give Jonathan something he could eat. After a mere two weeks at home since his diagnosis, Jonathan had reached the point where he could not eat a normal home cooked meal anymore. He was consuming soft foods like yoghurt and rice puddings – often giving me a shopping list of foods he felt he could eat before then abandoning it as his condition got worse. I cannot remember the number of times I went up and down the stairs – tending to both Jonathan one minute and then the boys the next. All the while trying to keep my own feelings of despair under check. I did this all on my own – no family members to help, no friends to assist. The truth was I did not have any really close friends around me. And as for my mother and sister, well, they had never been the type to offer assistance when I really needed it even as they were aware of how bad the situation was, and the chaotic circumstances I was in meant there was little opportunity to sit down and have a frank heart to heart about it. As I had done in the past when navigating difficult periods whilst married to Jonathan, I developed a bunker mentality in order to just keep going – very similar to one I had adopted whilst going through challenging times during my officer training in the RAF. *You are in stretch – but you can do it, keep going,* I told myself. But although I did, fuelled at times by pride and not much else, I still felt alone. And burnt out.

As Jonathan's condition rapidly deteriorated I began to realise that I could not cope with looking after him – not just because I was looking after the boys as well – but because Jonathan was becoming far too ill too quickly. The simple paracetamol and codeine he had were no match for the pain he was feeling. I firmly believe that two weeks after his diagnosis Jonathan needed to be in hospital. I don't recall if I ever explicitly broached this with him, but if I had there was no doubt that Jonathan would have objected strenuously: his dislike of attending hospitals as a patient would have quelled any cooperation on that front. But something had to be done. I had no idea what I was doing. I simply did not have enough medical knowledge to care for him effectively while we waited for the next stage in the appointment cycle.

I decided on my mother's advice to reach out to his brother for help. I debated the issue, reluctant to speak to him given the frosty reception I had received from him a couple of weeks ago. On the other hand, I was desperate: Jonathan may not listen to me but he was likely to listen to his brother. So in the early evening, a week before my husband died, I called Tom and voiced my concerns.

'Jonathan is very ill. I really think he needs to go into hospital.' I spoke quietly in the kitchen not wanting the boys to hear above the din of the TV in the living room.

'Why? Did he say that?'

'No, he doesn't want to go but he is so weak and is in a lot of pain. He just seems to be getting worse and worse. I think he needs proper medical care.'

Tom paused. 'OK. Let me speak to him.'

I was relieved. I went upstairs and handed my phone to Jonathan. I really thought that Tom would help me, maybe realising that I would not be saying this if I was not concerned. Tom then spoke to Jonathan, whilst I went back downstairs. After a short while I went back into the bedroom and Jonathan handed the phone back to me with an air of impatience. I did not know what that meant but I hoped that Tom had spoken some sense into him. I went back into the kitchen and closed the door.

'Well I've spoken to him.' Tom's voice was unemotional.

'I'm satisfied that Jonathan doesn't need to go into hospital.' I was stunned.

What a slap in the face that was.

Tom had ignored me.

He had disregarded my opinion. Instead, he had chosen to listen to my stubborn husband, the patient whose perspective would be completely clouded by illness. He may well have had good cause to not argue with Jonathan at the time but at the very least, I would have expected him to say that he would come and visit his brother and see for himself.

But he did not.

Tom's latent hostility and lack of respect towards me was deeply upsetting but at the time I just absorbed this. I had no power over the situation and I was utterly depleted. I put the issue to one side. *Not now.*

A few days after this conversation with Tom, during the weekend, he and Patricia finally did come. Except that it was not quite the support that I was expecting. It did not help that when I opened the door to them the first thing that Patricia said was, 'The cavalry have arrived!' If only. As they came into the house, Patricia looked around at the walls and the ceiling, the clutter in the hallway and living room as though for the first time, muttering to Tom 'Yes, it's a mess.' I gritted my teeth, resisting the temptation to slam the front door shut after they crossed the threshold.

The 'cavalry' ended up delighting Jonathan but upsetting me deeply in the process. The first notable thing about the 'cavalry' was that they had arrived wielding duvets and pillows – items which we already had in our home but of course would not be deemed good enough for Jonathan. The fact that it was Jonathan who had requested these items from his mother should not have surprised me – but it did.

Tom and Patricia then went into the bedroom to see Jonathan. I left them alone. They then came downstairs. Patricia moved into the kitchen with me.

'Look, at everything he wanted. He wanted rice puddings, so I got them and then he wanted custards and I got them – anything he wanted I went and got it!' I started throwing open the cupboards to show her all the food items I had bought for Jonathan – the untouched tubs of rice puddings, custards and other similar items spilling out of the shelves. I was in tears. I stopped abruptly but continued crying.

'I know, I know Thelma, I can see all you have done.' Patricia said the right words but she did so in a reserved manner, patting my shoulder awkwardly before going upstairs to see Jonathan again. At a loss, I went into the living room. Tom was there with Dominic and Richard. I sat down on the couch and placed Richard on my lap.

'Have you spoken to the boys about Jonathan?' Tom's tone was neutral. He was unmoved by my tears.

I gave a desperate shrug. I felt depressed. I felt exhausted. It was not my finest hour – my resilience had completely abandoned me. Following my tearful 'non response' there was no recognition of the agony I was in from Tom.

He turned to Dominic to speak to him. He moved closer and knelt in front of him.

'I am very sad about your daddy. I'm sure you must be upset too.' Tom wiped away a tear to demonstrate. I was shocked. This was the first time that I had actually seen him cry about Jonathan.

'You see, it's OK to be upset and to cry.' Dominic watched him with big eyes, obviously in awe of him. Tom continued to say reassuring things to him before he then went upstairs to see Jonathan again. That small snippet of time that he spent talking to Dominic was actually quite good for my son. There was obviously a caring side to Tom. It was just not a side that I had access to.

Having Tom and Patricia in my home, at Jonathan's behest, was bad enough. But combined with them also treating me with what I felt was an underlying contempt was in the end too much for me to bear.

I had to leave the house.

But first I had to wait for my mother to arrive. I had called my mother and asked her to come as soon as I knew my in-laws were visiting. I'd wanted her here for moral support more than anything else. But she was late. As usual. My impatience grew with each minute that went by. As soon as she came I left the house and took Richard with me. Dominic was I think quite enamoured with having Tom around and wanted to stay so I left him behind under the care of my mother. Richard and I got in the car and drove literally five minutes to the bottom of my road. I parked the car in front of Roundwood park and just sat there with Richard.

I was shaking with rage and despair.

I cannot remember how long I left the house for, it must have been at least an hour or two. Towards the end of my time in self-imposed exile I rang my mother to find out how my eldest son was getting on. My mother told me that Dominic had just been following Tom around, clearly impressed with having his uncle around. Tom however, had seemed largely uninterested in him. This upset me quite a lot. Now I felt torn. I knew I should head back but I simply could not bring myself to be in the same space as them. As the light started to fade and Richard became restless, I realised I had no choice. With a great deal of reluctance I returned to the house just as they were about to leave. As Tom came down the stairs moving towards the front door I stopped him.

'Did you manage to do everything you needed?'

Tom avoided my eyes and gave a cryptic answer: 'I was just following Jonathan's instructions.'

What an odd response. I could not think of an appropriate reply so I said nothing. I soon found out why he was behaving in such a defensive manner.

When I came into Jonathan's room he was beaming. That was the first time I had seen him close to happy since his diagnosis. Perhaps even longer, way before he got ill. And the source of it was his mother and his brother. Not his wife. I put that thought to one side. *Not now.*

When Jonathan and I had discussed Tom and Patricia's visit, we had agreed that Tom could help with a few practical matters such as moving Richard's cot bed from the spare room into Dominic's room so the boys could share one room. This would have allowed Jonathan to stay in the spare bedroom on his own and give him the privacy that he needed while he was so ill. I thought that that was the extent of the practical help that Tom was providing.

Wrong again.

As I moved from Jonathan's room into the master bedroom (effectively my bedroom now) I stopped in my tracks as I walked in through the door. While I had been out of the house with Richard, it seemed that Jonathan had given further 'instructions' to Tom and Patricia to do far more than what we had discussed. The reclining chair had been moved from the living room into our bedroom and was now opposite me, occupying new space in my room. Other pieces of furniture in my room had been moved slightly or adjusted. So Patricia and Tom had rearranged not just the spare room but also the master bedroom. *My room, my personal space.* I couldn't believe it – I was speechless. This was not the worst of it however. The rearranging of furniture was bad enough, but as I slowly did a full circle and carefully surveyed my room I saw the full extent of their handiwork. Patricia had gone through my wardrobe, taken out some of my clothes and hung them on the outside of the closet. I would later learn that Tom had also relocated some of my personal items, including my hair pieces and accessories. I only discovered this weeks later after I had conducted a search for them and found that they had been placed in the lockers at the bottom of my garden. Upon discovering them stuffed there I had broken down in tears and cried for a very long time in my bedroom stifling the noise into my pillow so my boys could not hear. However, that was to come much later. For now, as I stood in my bedroom staring at the nightgown that Patricia had taken from my wardrobe and hung on a hanger I felt shocked and bewildered. How could they have done this?

And why had Jonathan let them?

I knew that Jonathan had wanted us to declutter for a long time – so he had clearly used Tom's presence to do all the things that he had wanted to do but couldn't. But surely Tom and Patricia would have known that this was a violation of my privacy? *How could they do this? How?!* I could not believe the way I had been treated. And for what? What was my crime?

Why did this family hate me so much?

I felt betrayed.

I felt so very hurt.

Then just as quickly I felt a switch turn on inside me. In that moment my despair changed into a white hot anger. That was the beginning of my rage towards Jonathan's family.

As for Jonathan, I loathed him too at that point.

But it was a different story for my husband. That visit with his family was probably the highlight for Jonathan during these past few weeks since his diagnosis. The good mood he was in after their visit stayed with him for some time. However, this was only a brief respite: the cancer was still there. It continued to spread and Jonathan continued to deteriorate. He was soon in significant pain. And eating very little. Each soft food I brought up for him ended up being barely touched. As the October half term began, a mere day or so after his mother and brother had left, Jonathan took a turn for the worse. The night that would end up being Jonathan's last night at the house began like any other.

As I finished meal time with the children I received a text message on my phone. It was a text from Tom offering to help – something I felt should have been much more forthcoming ages ago. My initial relief at being offered help did not last however. Jonathan had an appointment to start his first chemotherapy very soon and I had up until that point been trying to figure out how to get him to this appointment at Hammersmith Hospital. Although I had arranged for Jonathan to have a porter and a wheelchair waiting for him once we reached the hospital car park, I had not yet managed to arrange for transportation to the hospital itself from our home. I asked Tom if he could help with that. Tom's response to me was immediate.

And cold.

He demanded that I call him saying that he needed more details. He went on stating that his impression was that Jonathan was not *'well enough to attend an outpatient chemo appointment on Thursday'*. After pointing out why it was unlikely Jonathan would be having chemotherapy he then ended abruptly with *'You haven't given me his team's information and I don't know who to contact, let alone whether you or he want me to get involved as an advocate.'*

No preamble.

No warmth.

I stared at the text for a little while reading and re-reading it. I then lost my temper. It was probably not fair because despite his obvious dislike of me he was actually offering some assistance. But, I was completely strung out and exhausted at the end of another long and very difficult day. I thought: *this man has the temerity to question me and patronise me and treat me like I am nothing!* I responded with fury:

> '*[Tom]. I have given you all the details that I have. Jonathan told me that he has a chemotherapy appointment on the Thursday – that's it. They called him while I was not in the room and I have not been able to find out [any] more information since then even though I have been trying. I am getting quite annoyed and upset with this insinuation that I am [not] doing enough! I have been the one screaming for more to happen until now – but which have all fallen on deaf ears! It is great that you want to help Jonathan – there is nothing stopping you as a doctor from calling Hammersmith yourself and helping to find out the information that I am trying in vain to find. There is nothing stopping you from calling Jonathan yourself in the morning to speak to him and find out. But what I will not stand for is being treated like some sort of imbecile after everything that I have been doing to look after Jonathan and the kids! I will send you the letter and the contact details for the oncology team and for the useless CNS nurse I can barely get hold of. You want to advocate for Jonathan and help? – there you go – you will have the details – go off and do it.'*

In any given night, my furious exchanges with Tom would be enough to round off a thoroughly miserable evening. However, it seems that that night was only getting started.

An hour or so after my tense text messages with his brother, I brought Jonathan some food. I watched as Jonathan attempted to eat some strawberries which he had requested. They were soft fruits so he thought he could manage to eat them. He managed very little. Before I went to bed, I went to check on him. I collected the bowl of strawberries which were untouched and paused to look at him. Jonathan was sleeping, looking uncomfortable as he stretched out on the bed. I crept out quietly and let him rest. I thought I was in for a quiet night. About 30 minutes later, I heard Jonathan next door, sounding like he was in pain. When I went in Jonathan was in a bad state, he was throwing up what looked like red liquid on the floor. At first I mistook it for the strawberries he had attempted to eat – but it wasn't strawberries – it was blood. He had started coughing up blood. I knew then that regardless of what Jonathan believed, he needed hospital care.

'I need to get you into hospital!'

'No, I don't want to go into hospital.'

'But you are coughing up blood!'

'I don't want to go!' Jonathan's face was defiant. If he was fearful, that fear was submerged well below the surface. What I saw in front of me was a man drawing battle lines prepared for a long, *long* fight.

I looked at the carpet, stained red with the blood my husband had just thrown up. In that moment, I made up my mind. Ignoring Jonathan's wishes, I called an ambulance. Even in his weakened state, he glared at me with deep annoyance as I dialled 999. I continued to ignore him. I was not going to give in to the wishes of a man who was literally dying before my very eyes.

When the ambulance crew came, I asked them to be quiet going up to the first floor to avoid waking the boys. I was grateful as they made their way carefully up the creaking stairs. They came into the room where Jonathan was waiting. Even in the pitiful state he was in his stubbornness was etched out on his face and in his body language. He clearly was not going down without a fight. I turned to the ambulance crew and spoke to them at length – explaining Jonathan's condition in some detail. I may have ended by saying that he needed to go into hospital but I would have thought that was obvious. The ambulance crew spoke to him whilst checking his vital signs and indicated that they were happy to take him into hospital. It was then that my husband revealed the full extent of his pigheadedness. With eyes barely open from exhaustion and his body still in the most fragile state, Jonathan stood as rigid as he could and said:

'I have full capacity. I do not want to go into hospital.'

The ambulance crew tried to convince him to change his mind but this was to no avail. Jonathan clearly knew what he needed to do and say in order to get his own way about not going into hospital. The ambulance crew left. They effectively had no choice – they could not take him in without his consent.

I let them out and came back into the room. I was weary. I was tired of Jonathan. Tired of fighting him all the time – even on the issue of saving his life. I told him quietly, 'I'm going to bed.' And I left the room.

In the early hours of the morning I was awoken again. The retching noise coming from next door sounded alien but had also become increasingly familiar as the night wore on. I went next door to find Jonathan crouched over the bed, his head in the waste bin basket, coughing up blood again. The awful state the illness had left him in was unmistakeable. This time I did not debate with him. I told him firmly that I was calling the ambulance again. Jonathan still resisted but even he could not deny the reality of the situation: he needed hospital care. I suppose in Jonathan's mind he could relent but only if he could have some sort of win or vindication. That win turned out to be the choice of hospital. When the second ambulance crew arrived he did not welcome them. He turned to me:

'I will go but only if they take me to Charing Cross Hospital.'

'I don't know if they are allowed to do that!'

'I only want to go to Charing Cross Hospital.'

So I tried. I pleaded with the ambulance people to take Jonathan to the hospital of his choice. I advocated for my dying husband in a way that I had not done in a long time. I was still his wife, he was still the father of my children and I needed, and wanted to do the best for him. The ambulance crew eventually agreed. They made a call seeking permission to take him to Charing Cross Hospital and after it was granted he was taken there. I have no doubt in my mind, as I helped him to get dressed and put his jaundiced feet into his shoes, my husband would not have gotten in that ambulance van if the destination was not to his liking – even if it had led to his immediate death. As he got into that ambulance, a mere 18 days after his diagnosis, it did not occur to me at the time that this would be the last time that Jonathan would see his house again or that I would have my husband in my house with me. This was the beginning of the end of our time together.

CHAPTER 5

The Hospital

Jonathan had gone into the ambulance in the early hours of the morning. I then had a decision to make: do I go to the hospital with Jonathan and take the kids with me or do I drop the kids off at half-term camp so they are out of the way for the day and I can focus on Jonathan without having to cater to the kids etc? Not having anyone else on hand to help, not feeling that I could call on anyone else was an awful feeling. It made me feel lonely.

And helpless.

I decided on the latter. That meant that I had only a few hours to organise the boys and take them to the camp which I had thankfully booked in advance. As soon as I dropped them off I would then go to the hospital.

As I busied myself sorting out the kids I received a text from Tom. He had cancelled his patient list and had decided to come to London. He had called Jonathan who had informed him of where he was and now Tom was making his way to Charing Cross Hospital to meet me there.

I felt numb as I drove my boys to the half-term camp based in Hampstead Heath, my mind completely paralysed. I would soon be joining their father in hospital and I dreaded having to deal with what came next. At the same time, whilst interacting with my boys, I had to put on a mask, take on the persona of someone feeling extremely calm and secure in the future and the fact that their father was in hospital was actually quite normal and nothing to be alarmed about.

'Where is Daddy?' Dominic asked the question whilst looking out of the window.

'You know that Daddy is not well. Daddy was feeling very poorly so he is now in hospital where he can get some help.'

'When is he coming back?'

'Hopefully soon.'

I love my children very much but truth be told it was a relief to be able to drop them off and be able to take off the mask. I cried silent tears as I drove home to park the car before leaving for the hospital.

When I reached the hospital, Tom and June were there waiting. Jonathan was clearly in a bad way and was already on the A&E ward with a room and a bed. I went to see him and a young male doctor was tending to him. The doctor was talking a lot of medical jargon which of course Jonathan understood. Even at that stage Jonathan was trying to direct and control the situation by firing questions at the young doctor and giving his own input. This was typical of Jonathan. I found it consoling in a way. Jonathan was still Jonathan. How bad could it be? We had to wait for the oncologist to come and whilst that occurred I excused myself to go and make a call. I realised that Jonathan was going to be at the hospital for a while which meant that I had absolutely no childcare for the whole of the half term – I had only booked the boys' camp for one day – I had not anticipated that I would be in this position. So I called the camp that the boys were at and managed to book them in for several more days. I felt detached whilst in the hospital garden, entering an almost dreamlike state as I made the arrangements – similar to the state I had entered when Jonathan and I were leaving St Mary's Hospital after the diagnosis. I was floating in my mind. Struggling to catch up with reality whilst wanting to run away from it at the same time. For Jonathan's sake however, I was also relieved to be there – finally I had some serious help in taking care of him – not having the sole burden fall on me.

When I went back inside the oncologist had already arrived. She had just been speaking to Jonathan with Tom and June also present. Tom and June then went to the waiting room. I was left with the doctor and Jonathan. I was already limbering up, wondering if I could persuade her to help me arrange the transportation to Jonathan's first chemotherapy treatment at Hammersmith hospital. Even though events had moved on, like a comfort blanket, I had gone back to trying to solve a problem that probably no longer existed. The oncologist was an Asian woman with a calm and pleasant manner. Like a broken record in my head the chanting which had started as soon as I had arrived at the hospital grew louder: *this is not real, this is not happening, this is not real, this is not happening …* Mentally I shook myself. I looked at the doctor. *Get a grip.* 'So what happens now? What's the prognosis?'

Silence.

I tried again. 'He has a chemotherapy session in two days on Thursday.'

This time the doctor answered. Slowly. Carefully. 'We are just going to make sure he is comfortable.'

'What do you mean? Is he not going to receive any treatment from the hospital?'

'We think it's best to just make him as comfortable as possible.'

Oh.

Oh.

It finally hit home.

Jonathan was too far gone.

He would not be leaving the hospital. Not now. Not ever. I gestured to her that I wanted to speak to her outside. Once we were alone I turned back to her. This was too much reality for me right now. But the door had been opened and I had no choice but to move towards to it. I knew the words I was going to say but that did not make it any easier as I braced myself and said them.

'How long?'

As before, the doctor did not answer immediately. Like a bulldozer, I ploughed on:

'Months?'

She hesitated slightly then said cautiously 'Anytime soon.'

'Days? Weeks?'

'Maybe.'

The doctor was kind, full of empathy. I could see it in her face, in her warm eyes. I am glad that she indulged me and gave me a soft landing. Because I was not ready to fully accept what was happening. Not just then.

I went into the waiting room where Tom and June were and promptly burst into tears. They consoled me – of course they already knew. I blamed myself saying that it was my fault. They told me it was not my fault but of course I did not believe them. In that moment we all forgot the different positions we had taken and were united in our grief. I felt for an instant that I was not alone in all this – that Jonathan's family were here too on the same journey as me. I wish that feeling could have lasted.

಄   ಄   ಄

Jonathan ended up being in hospital for three days – from Tuesday 22 October 2019 to Friday 26 October 2019. I remained in a daze throughout that time. Tom and June's presence at the hospital was in some ways a very good thing – they understood the medical terminology, they understood the politics of it all and were able to advocate for Jonathan on medical matters in a way that I never could, ensuring that he was getting the right care, being shifted onto the right ward at the right time and so on. And yes I do recall June offering at least once to go home and help look after the kids whilst I stayed at the hospital.

The first time she had offered to do so was when I had been about to leave to pick up the boys from camp after Jonathan's first day at the hospital:

'I could go home and look after the boys whilst you stay here with Jonathan. I don't mind honestly.' We were in the hospital corridor. I think Tom had gone to get some drinks so it was just June and I. She seemed sincere, maybe even concerned, holding her eye contact with me as she spoke. I did think about it briefly. But in the end I declined.

There were a number of reasons – stubbornness I suppose – I have not always been good at receiving help and I suppose saying yes would be an admission of some sort of failure. There was also the fact that I wanted to be in control of my space and environment and I did not relish the prospect of someone that I did not know well or trusted enough being in that space, especially after what had happened the last time I had left my house in the hands of my in-laws. I was also conscious of the fact that I wanted the boys to operate as normal as possible and having June there would be the opposite of normal and would add to the boys' heightened sense of anxiety. In any case there was a need for me to keep my distance from them – after all they had not up until now been allies. So I said no, and spent the mornings dropping off the boys at camp and then spending the day at the hospital before going to pick up the boys and take them home and look after them until the next morning, when I would do the same again. By contrast, Tom and June stayed at the hospital primarily doing the evening and night shifts when they took over from me.

Very shortly after my talk with the oncologist, June suggested that Jonathan needed supplies as he was going to be staying in the hospital for a while. I had not even thought of that – such was my shock. So I went out to the neighbouring high street where there was a plethora of shops. I went into Marks and Spencer to buy my dying husband some pyjamas, trying to figure out the sizing and what would fit him now given his significant weight loss. On the one hand, I was trying to make decisions about things such as socks, underwear – what size, how much etc. and on the other hand realising it was all futile and that this would all be meaningless in the long term. I watched other shoppers going about their business, marvelling at how normal everything was and yet knowing that everything was as abnormal, as strange and as wrong as it could possibly be. I was floating – like a ghost. I was present and at the same time I was not present. Carrying on as normal even while my world was quietly crashing down.

I felt in many ways like an imposter during the time that I was in the hospital. Even though I was Jonathan's wife, I did not feel that I had ownership of the process of looking after him. When Jonathan was on the ward waiting to be moved to another bed, a nurse had come to help with cleaning him. Jonathan had insisted that I do it and of course I had obliged but I had felt detached whilst doing it. I wonder if that was a consequence of the fact that our marriage had been difficult and it felt disingenuous to be the doting wife and for Jonathan to cast me as such. Or perhaps it was just as likely that I was in the process of shutting down. Having held the fort for so long on my own I had come to the end of what I could reasonably contribute. I was also grateful to have some respite – to have others worry about Jonathan's care and make all the decisions that seemed to flummox me in the past when I had sole care of looking after him.

In addition to myself, Tom and June, Jonathan had others that came, especially when it became apparent that Jonathan's time was fast approaching. My mother came down to see him and stayed with him for a bit. The boys also came to visit Jonathan. Dominic was wearing the outfit that Jonathan had worn as a boy many years ago. I did not want him to wear it as I wanted it to be preserved and not get tarnished in any way but Jonathan had disagreed – saying, 'let him wear it if he wants to.' By the time Valerie had brought them to the hospital Jonathan was very weak, barely awake and heavily sedated for the pain. He was also in some form of denial about his condition. The oncologist was in the room when the boys came and Jonathan expressed concern at having the boys there because they could bring disease or germs which could compromise him. The doctor assured him it was fine: the implication being of course that it was rather too late for all that. I look back now and I do think that it was important that the boys were there and had an opportunity to say goodbye because often times, years afterwards they would ask me about Jonathan's final days and I am able to say that they were there and were able to say goodbye to their father.

Patricia and Vincent eventually came as well. And when they did I felt pushed out. I remember Tom sending a text to me that his parents wanted to see Jonathan now as the wheelchair provided to Vincent would be needed by another person soon. So myself and the boys had to leave the room whilst Patricia and Vincent went in. One or both of the boys went to greet Patricia and she absent-mindedly patted them on the head but paid them no mind after that. It felt as if we, as in me and the boys were separate from them and we had to leave to make way for the 'important' family members. It would also explain why when Patricia, Vincent, Tom and June were sitting in the waiting room of the hospital, I did not join them. We were not one big happy family and I felt a complete outsider – it was a matter of them and me. I sat alone.

Over the course of Jonathan's last days in hospital, he was also seen by his work colleagues. The first colleague to come up and see him was his fellow doctor and consultant David. His name came up during one of the more morbid conversations that Jonathan and I had when he was first brought to the hospital: that of his death and the aftermath. I can barely remember how we started the conversation nor the words actually spoken. I do remember how I felt – numb and overwhelmed but trying to be efficient, broaching the subject with hesitancy whilst on the constant brink of tears. By stark contrast Jonathan was very matter of fact about it – characteristically direct and brief in his responses. Jonathan made it clear that he wanted a funeral in a big church like the church I attended. His instructions were that all his patients who wanted to attend should attend. His colleague David was to be tasked with ensuring that all those patients would be contacted and told to come. I was in a taxi, on my way to the hospital on the second day after Jonathan had been admitted when I made the call. I took care when I told David about Jonathan's diagnosis and the true reason that Jonathan had not been at work. I could feel his shock after I had uttered the words.

'Oh no, oh no, that's awful.' David broke off, his voice cracking. He fell silent.

Jonathan often spoke about David, as his fellow ally when it came to certain medical issues and in other cases as an irritant who frustrated him from time to time. It was clear that there was something in their relationship that was akin to brotherly rivalry and love. David was now losing Jonathan – his colleague and friend that he had known for many years. And in the most devastating way. It was no surprise he was so upset.

'I'm sorry David.' I paused, giving him a chance to catch his breath.

'Is he at the hospital now? I would really like to see him Thelma.' I initially resisted. Jonathan had made it clear that he did not want his work colleagues to visit him at the hospital. However, David would not have it:

'Please Thelma, I would really, really like to see him. This has been such a shock, I really do need to see him.' I tried to let him know about Jonathan's wish for privacy but David was insistent. In the end, I told him that I would ask Jonathan. When I relayed my conversation with David to Jonathan later he rolled his eyes – he obviously saw David's visit as completely unnecessary – in complete contrast to David whose tearful plea was so moving. Eventually, Jonathan relented and David was able to visit him, thanking me later for managing to persuade Jonathan to change his mind.

※   ※   ※

It is remarkable that even at this late stage of his life, whilst in hospital, the very place he did not want to be, Jonathan was largely unsentimental and unmoved by the situation. The way that he was able to talk about his funeral arrangements with an air of detachment. Or the way that he insisted that I take his laptop (which he had made sure to carefully pack) put it on and then proceed to send his research project (the same project that he had been working on in one form or another throughout the whole time that I had known him) to various players in the medical world to ensure that the work he had done would be carried on by one of his colleagues. This probably should not have been a priority at the time. But Jonathan was running the show then, and doing his bidding made me feel useful and connected to him in a way that was not always possible with us.

The day before Jonathan died, he fell into a coma after receiving a new cancer treatment. This had been offered by one of the oncologists a day after we had arrived at the hospital. It would be risky but if it worked it came with significant benefits. Jonathan and I had discussed it and decided that he should try this new experimental blood transfusion and chemotherapy. The purpose of the treatment was to try to alleviate his pain and possibly give him some more time – maybe several weeks. The doctor made it clear that the chances of it working was not high: it could make him feel better but it could also make him feel much, much worse. At the same time, almost vying in the opposite direction, was the palliative care team wanting to discuss his palliative care going forward. The palliative care consultant was disappointed when Jonathan decided to try this treatment, expressing his view that it was unlikely to work. However, in making the decision, Jonathan and I were both united (I think) in feeling that despite everything it was worth the risk – our human survival instinct asserting itself. After all, what did we have to lose? It was certainly in keeping with the kind of doctor that Jonathan was, the kind who was never afraid to take such risks.

Before Jonathan began this treatment and became too heavily sedated to communicate, we did have a final conversation. Tom and June were waiting outside the hospital room when I came in to see Jonathan. He looked so forlorn, weak and ill. I cried as I hugged him. I can't remember what I said to him or if I even said anything at all as I gave over to the wave of despair and grief which overcame me. The last thing he said to me was 'You are so sweet.' I kissed his hand. When we parted I did not think that that would be the last conversation that we would ever have.

But it was.

Because in the end the palliative doctor was right, it absolutely did not work. Jonathan never regained consciousness and never recovered. His deterioration carried on at a rapid pace following the failed treatment until it was too late for anything other than the inevitable.

The last few hours of his life were like a whirlwind. We were eventually told in the afternoon of 25 October 2019 that Jonathan did not have much time – he was likely to die that night. Patricia immediately started giving instructions, telling me: 'You will stay here.' There were so many moments that I would look back on later that would fill me with a silent fury. Without a doubt that was one of those moments. What was Patricia thinking of? Telling the wife of a dying man that she should stay with him? Of course I was going to do that! But the implication of what she said and meant was clear: *I should stay because it was not apparent that I would stay because I clearly had not been devoted enough to being with Jonathan.* And that was the crux of the issue: no matter what I did, how much I drove myself mad trying to look after my dying husband and our three year old and a six year old children – it would never be good enough. Never. However, this would be an argument for another day. For now, the waves of shock and grief were continuing and making me numb.

I said nothing.

I now had to deal (again) with the practicalities of the situation. I would not be going home this evening and I needed to arrange childcare for the boys. I contacted Valerie and asked her, no, begged her to help. However, she could not – she was babysitting that night. I remember feeling outrage that this should take precedence over a dying man but of course this was absurd. As close as Valerie was to us – she had her own life, she was not actually family even though it felt like it the vast majority of the time. This was not her responsibility. Nonetheless she helped me to find someone, another nanny I had seen in passing but never used before called Penny, who could babysit the boys until later that evening. I contacted my mother and arranged for her to take over from Penny and stay with the boys overnight. Having sorted out the childcare arrangements, I drifted back into Jonathan's room and stayed there watching him. The whole room, the whole event playing out like a never-ending nightmare. I could not be sure that it was real, that I was actually here, that Jonathan was in that hospital bed with the life seeping out of him. Was it only two months ago that we were all in France, going on a pedalo journey, visiting a bamboo farm, enjoying the pool in the gite that we were staying in? *How could this be happening?*

A knock on the door, and a nurse popped her head inside. 'I'm sorry, but there are some people outside who want to talk to you. They say that they worked with your husband.'

I went outside and saw a black man and a black woman and one other but I cannot recall who now. The first two I would later recognise as Michael and Amaka, a nurse and pharmacist who worked with Jonathan at the hospital. No doubt David had informed his colleagues and word had spread. Jonathan was close to his last moments. I tried to tell them that this was not a good time and that this was not the time for visitors. However, they insisted that they see Jonathan before it was too late. I saw the tears in their eyes and how overcome with emotion they were: Jonathan clearly meant a lot to them. I would find out later just how well regarded and treasured Jonathan was by his colleagues. For now, I nodded and allowed them to spend time with Jonathan. After they had seen him, they thanked me profusely. They looked heartbroken as they left but were clearly relieved that they were able to say their goodbyes.

I felt drained. I could feel the world closing in on me. I needed space. I could not go into the waiting room occupied by Patricia et al. I could not face them. Their hostility towards me was like a vague mist hanging in the air – unformed and sketchy but nevertheless making its presence felt: I knew I was not welcome there. I went out into the lobby and sat in front of the lifts. As I was sitting there I was joined by the oncologist. He was the doctor that had been fleeting but kind. He had checked on Jonathan's condition and had been the one to gently allow the boys to see Jonathan despite Jonathan's protests to the contrary – clearly recognising that Jonathan had not fully absorbed the extent of his illness at that stage. As I had him all to myself, I decided to ask him what had been going round in my mind since this nightmare had all started.

'I don't understand how the cancer could have spread so quickly?'

'The cancer would have been there for a long time.'

'How long?'

'At least a year before. He would have had very few symptoms. Bile duct cancer often presents late and by the time it does it's normally too late. I've dealt with many cases like this.' He nodded at the wards leading off to one side of the corridor. 'Actually, I have a couple of patients in rooms just over there – in broadly the same situation as Jonathan – cancer presenting late, too late for any real intervention.'

'There was a Wellman screening that I had tried to get Jonathan to do but he didn't want to and I didn't insist. Is it my fault? Could I have prevented it?'

'No, no absolutely not.' He paused. 'The cancer would have been very hard to detect in the initial stages. This was not your fault.'

The theme of fault is something that would continue to haunt me in the weeks and months following Jonathan's death. The fact that in some way it was my fault, that I caused it. I would ask myself later whether this was some variation of survivor's guilt – perhaps it was. Twisting its way inside my thought process and slowly strangling all rational explanations for Jonathan's illness. This was something I would revisit time and time again. But at this stage the belief that I was to blame in some way was overwhelming. So despite what the doctor said I dismissed it in my head. I thought *You are so, so wrong.*

I went back into the room to be with Jonathan. Tom and June were in there. Patricia and Vincent joined us and we all stayed there together by Jonathan's bed. I cannot remember how long we waited, if we spoke or what the sequence of events were but at some point June felt Jonathan's pulse and indicated that it was very weak – it would soon be time. When Jonathan had passed over I cried. I stroked his face saying repeatedly, '*I will find you, I will find you.*' And then he was gone.

Tom cried, comforted by June. Vincent cried comforted by Patricia.

It was all over.

⚘ ⚘ ⚘

Jonathan was gone.

It was a relief to know that he was no longer in pain. The last day or so when he was at the hospital, although heavily sedated, Jonathan would indicate from time to time that he was in pain and he would then be given more pain relief. What an awful hell he must have gone through. One of the things that Patricia would constantly say was 'He must not feel any pain!' Well, that wish had now come true – Jonathan was beyond pain now. He was beyond this existence. He had left us and in doing so had taken with him my sole purpose for being at the hospital.

I cannot recall how we made our way down to the ground floor of the hospital but the next thing I remember we were all there – stunned and in my case numb and weary. I wanted to go home. I was intending to get a taxi and do just that. I felt weird like I was at a loose end. I had been expecting to be at the hospital all night. But in the end, mercifully for Jonathan, he had passed peacefully and quickly. The journey for him was over. Mine as a widow was only just beginning.

'Tom can give you a lift,' June offered. I demurred but she insisted. Given how detached I felt from them I had wanted desperately to be on my own, to start piecing together what had happened. To start making sense of this nightmare. I needed solitude to do this. However, she had offered and it seemed churlish to turn down the ride home. Besides which, given the trauma of the night maybe it was best not to be left alone. Not yet anyway.

During the ride home Tom and I talked about Jonathan and how he had been up until the very end. Tom spoke with admiration for his brother: in awe of the fact that until the very end Jonathan had wanted to do things his way. He also talked about June, how amazing he thought she had been during this crisis. It was clear that he loved his wife very much. I was reminded in that moment of the partnership, imperfect as it was, that I had just lost – I was no longer part of a couple anymore: I was now on my own.

I began to feel anxious as we neared home. I had been expecting to arrive home much, much later than this. Given the time, Richard was unlikely to be awake. The same could not be said for Dominic. I fervently hoped that he was asleep. I could not face him. We arrived at my house. Tom turned to me.

'Well I am sorry for your loss.' I remember at the time thinking it was an odd thing to say to me – something I would expect from a stranger, not from someone who had also lost his only brother – surely Jonathan's death was his loss as well?

'I am sorry for your loss too,' I managed.

'Is it OK if we come over to the house tomorrow?'

'Yes of course.'

I said this convincingly but I actually did not want them to come. I needed space. I wanted to be alone with my boys. However, I imagined that they wanted to come together and grieve and show support. So feeling obligated I gave Tom the response that he wanted and pushed my feelings aside.

When I came in, Penny was on the sofa watching TV. The place was messier than I liked but any irritation I felt was quelled by the wave of sadness and sorrow that I suddenly felt.

Penny said, 'How are you love? Has he gone?'

I nodded and then the tears came. Penny kindly hugged me. Up until that point I had not known Penny well at all. I had seen her around a lot in my neighbourhood but she was really a stranger. How kind she was, to give up her time on short notice to babysit the children whilst I stayed at the hospital. And how kind she was now to hug me whilst I cried, feeling the grief and pain that I had locked away whilst in the car with Tom, not quite trusting myself to let go in front of him.

'Mummy?'

I turned and saw Dominic and felt dread seep through me. How I had hoped he would be sound asleep so I could gather myself and prepare to tell him and his brother the worst in the morning. I would have to face him now.

'Where is Daddy? Is he dead?'

I opened my mouth to answer but no words came out. In my mind's eye I saw myself speaking and telling my son that his father was gone. But in reality I was frozen. I could not speak. I could not say the words.

'Is he dead Mummy?'

I brought Dominic close and hugged him but I stayed silent, with tears still streaking down my face. Dominic wriggled out of the hug to look at me. He asked again.

It was Penny who answered. 'Yes lovey, Daddy is gone.'

Dominic's eyes widened and he shook his head 'No, no Mummy, is he really dead?' I hugged him again and murmured sorry over and over as Dominic started to cry.

Sometimes people come into your life at a certain point for a specific reason. Penny admitted to me later that same night that she had lost her mother at the age of nine – so she had a special understanding of the situation, of what I was going through, what the boys were going through, of a family that been traumatised beyond measure. So I will always be grateful to Penny for that night. For having the strength to tell Dominic what had happened to his father because at that moment I did not have the strength to do it. I was exhausted. I was spent. I wanted to crawl away and not face the next day and what came next.

Unfortunately, I would have to do just that.

CHAPTER 6

The Aftermath

The next day, the first day after my husband had died was the first day of the second chapter of my new life – my new life as a widow. That chapter began with the arrival of my in-laws. As promised, they all came into my house: Vincent, Patricia, Tom and June. Thankfully my mother was there also. Although no longer needed for the night shift, she arrived promptly in the morning and I was relieved that she came. For what should have been a moment of coming together with the whole family supporting each other did not quite transpire that way.

As they came into my house and settled themselves on my battered and old furniture I caught the familiar layer of unease that I always felt whenever my in-laws were close by. Even though I was newly widowed the element of hostility emanating from them was still there. I braced myself as I closed the front door. *It's fine, you can do this.*

Of all that were present in that room, the men, Tom and Vincent seemed the friendliest. Tom seemed almost relaxed. Vincent looked devastated. June and Patricia on the other hand were united in their distinct lack of empathy for me and in their anger – their body language and stiffness making this clear in waves.

My mother and I brought out the teas and then we sat down. My mother sat next to me, giving me some moral support by her proximity. It would be just her on my side of the family

– Dominic and Richard were not present. I cannot remember what I arranged for them but given the subject matter I had not wanted them around. It would be too much for them. It was too much for me, truth be told. But unlike them I had no choice in the matter.

'All these are Jonathan's?' Tom was looking at the array of sculptures and paintings that dotted the living room. He must have known the answer even as he asked but I guess he needed an ice breaker. I followed his gaze around the room taking in the art on display as though for the first time: the sculpture of the African man with exaggerated white marks near his eyes and the bust of an African woman sporting huge hoop earrings, and so many others, sculptures and paintings littered here and there casually around the room. There is no doubt – Jonathan is a talented artist. *Was* a talented artist.

'Yes.' I could not bring myself to say more.

'Would you mind if we take some paintings, some of his work to remember him by?'

'Yes of course, that's fine.' I felt numb.

The silence was often broken by Vincent who cried out spontaneously with grief for his son, the only person in the room showing authentic emotions at that time. He held out his hand at one point to me and I came to him. I had not always gotten on with Vincent but I felt a real connection to him that day.

After the initial small talk, the subject of the funeral was finally addressed. I talked to fill the space. It was delusional at the time but I felt this innate need to show that I was on top of things – that I had it all in hand. I told them that Jonathan and I had discussed funeral arrangements before he died and he had expressed his wish to be buried at my local church, the church I had attended on and off for the past several years (often without Jonathan). I would go through the list of Jonathan's contacts on his phone to tell his friends and others he knew about his death and to invite them to the funeral.

'Concerning other family members perhaps you could help with that – so that they can come to the funeral.'

'There is no one else, just us.' Patricia said this with a finality. 'Well, it looks like you have it all sorted and in hand.'

Despite her words there was no praise there. I tried to seek their opinion on whether Jonathan should be buried or cremated. My view was that those who wanted to be cremated normally made that extremely clear as it was such a specific thing to do. They did not seem bothered with Patricia just saying, 'Why don't you just bury him?' I pressed on.

'I don't have the funds to pay for the funeral now. Until the money from the estate comes through I will need help with the funeral costs.'

'Yes, that's fine.' In this Patricia was at least immediate in offering the financial help that I needed. The financial consequences of Jonathan's death had affected me quite badly. With separate bank accounts and no immediate access to his funds, I was, for the time being, in a very difficult financial position.

Patricia's firm offer of financial assistance was in direct contrast to the look that crossed June's face when I asked for help. June looked unhappy – her eyebrows raised and her expression soured. She looked away avoiding eye contact: her expression spoke volumes.

I felt wounded.

'I want that back!' Patricia pointed at a sculpture of a green disfigured head which was on the floor – her tone accusatory. It was an odd sculpture – showing a head turned in on itself in an impossible position. Jonathan always liked experimenting with abstract pieces. He had created the sculpture some time ago and had, I understand, given it to Patricia and Vincent. For reasons known only to Jonathan (he had never confided in me and I had never asked), he had taken back the sculpture, no doubt to protests from Patricia given her reaction now. In retrospect I wish I had said no to her request. After all, in order to honour Jonathan's wishes I probably should have kept it – for the boys at least. However, I lacked that insight. I was still in shock so course I said yes.

Then they left, with Tom toting the sculpture which Patricia had decided to appropriate and June leaving with a quick hug and the advice 'Just keep busy.' And that was that. My in-laws left and I did not see them again until at the funeral.

           ଧ   ଧ   ଧ

The leafy green area of West London that I live in is part of the locality fondly referred to as the 'Kensal Rise Triangle' which includes the area nestled between Kensal Rise, Kensal Green and Queen's Park. As well as being renowned for its many parks, great transport links and decent primary schools it also fostered a real community spirit. Although my kids were at the local primary school and there tends to be a *'Motherland'* type culture of parents who club together in this same spirit (and sometimes did so with what can only be described as unrestrained zeal), I had never really felt at that time that I was part of that culture. I was always missed out of the lunch or impromptu coffees and whereas I was now accustomed to it, initially it had bothered me. I suppose I have always operated on the outer fringes of normal social interactions and therefore it did not occur to me to turn to this community after Jonathan's death. To my surprise , I found some of this community on the first day back at school after Jonathan's death. I had debated with myself about taking the boys back to school a mere few days after Jonathan's death. Richard was an easy decision – he had not fully absorbed what had happened and a return to normality seemed like the best choice at the time. Dominic I was not so sure about. It made sense to give him the day off school. On the other hand, I did not have any childcare for him which I would need if he were to stay off school because I had the grim errand of collecting Jonathan's death certificate from the hospital. Under no circumstances did I want Dominic to accompany me whilst I carried out this task. So back to school it was and in a way it was the best thing for him at the time. He needed the formal structure of his usual routine – now more than ever – even if his world had collapsed around him.

We cried at the school gates, Dominic openly showing his grief and pain. I hugged him and let him cry. I ignored the looks I received and continued to hold him before he went into class.

I then turned my attention to Richard and started the journey towards College Green, his nursery. As I turned to walk I was stopped by Lucy, the class rep for Dominic's class.

'I am so sorry to hear about what has happened Thelma. Is there anything I can do?' Lucy had been friendly enough before but we were not close and I had always found her to be a bit stern looking. I knew she had been friendly with Jonathan and that they had seemed to get on quite well in the past.

'Thank you Lucy, I'm fine for now.' I took Richard's hand and started walking.

'Can I walk with you?' Even as she asked Lucy had already fallen into step with me.

'Thank you but there is no need.'

'Really I would like to.'

'Thank you, but really I'm fine.'

'Please, I would like to.'

She was certainly persistent. I was genuinely perplexed by her determination to walk with me to the nursery. Her insistence on talking to me and being there for me at that moment was in stark contrast to others on that first day back who had firmly kept their distance. I could not blame them – tragedies are hard to deal with at the best of times. Who knows what to say to someone whose husband has died a mere three weeks after diagnosis?

We did the walk up to College Green with Richard walking happily between us. I told her what had happened. It would be one of the many occasions when I would relate what had occurred over and over again.

Lucy's companionship on my first day back on the school run made me feel less lonely. In fact it was one of the many kindnesses bestowed upon me by the parent mums in that community. Although others continued to keep their distance, some parents eventually emerged, wishing me condolences either in person or by text, often offering to help in any way they could. I also received a collection from them – they had raised money for me which I was very touched by. It was also useful because I was very low on funds, being down to my last few hundred at that point. Jonathan's bank would not yet start giving me access to his accounts for a few weeks yet. There was also kindness in other forms, with Lucy and Kathy (Peter's mother) both surprising me by arriving at my home on separate occasions in the days and weeks after Jonathan had died with dishes that they prepared.

There was however, also complete bafflement from the parent mums too. They struggled to understand how I could be coping on my own. But most importantly, they seemed to think that once this kind of tragedy occurs, the woman will fall apart at the seams completely. This did not happen to me. Not initially anyway. I soldiered on throughout – combining visits to the law firm to sort out Jonathan's will with taking the children to school and nursery and then of course all their afterschool activities. I look back on it now and I do not blame them – what it must have seemed like for me to be marching my children to swimming to the point that I did not drop a swimming lesson. Actually, it was while I was at the swimming pool watching Dominic in his lesson a week or so after Jonathan's death that one parent mum stared at me in bewilderment when she saw me before asking me point blank: 'What are you doing here? If I lost my husband, I would be on the floor.' To which I had responded, 'If I stayed at home I wouldn't feel any better. Life goes on and the boys wanted to come.' I felt very calm and matter of fact during that exchange. But that was not enough to stop speculation about me. A week later, when I had returned to the same swimming pool for the boys' lessons, this time I found myself in company with Kathy and another mother. I chatted and joked with them as we all tried to navigate the onerous task of showering our children after their session in the water. It felt good to talk about other things and to act normal. As soon as I gathered my things and left, I could see from the corner of my eye, Kathy moving quickly to speak to the other mum in hushed tones. No prizes for guessing who she was talking about. I found that deeply annoying at the time even as I understood that this would be inevitable – the death of my husband would be gossip fodder for some time to come.

► ► ►

Jonathan's funeral took place four weeks after his death. Ordinarily it would have been sooner but I decided to delay by a week or so for a very good reason: Dominic's birthday. My sweet eldest child, now embarked on the awful journey of grief was soon to turn seven, a mere twenty days after his father's death. What an awful way to celebrate a birthday – with the shadow of his father's death in the background. It was just as well that I had never gotten round to planning a birthday party for him – it certainly would not be happening this year. Instead, we had a quiet celebration comprising of an exchange of gifts and a small cake. Lovely Valerie asked Dominic what he wanted and he had responded with goldfish – and true to her word, Valerie organised to take him and Richard to the local garden centre and set about dealing with the mechanics of buying a tank, fish and all the other paraphernalia needed to set up an aquatic home. She was truly kind and devoted to the boys – keeping them occupied and helping them (and me) just by being there for them in small but significant ways.

For my part, that four-week period between Jonathan's death and the funeral was hard to describe. Just as the other parent mums must have thought, I had always assumed as well that if I ever had to suffer the death of a loved one I would be distraught, and unable to function at all – sobbing into my pillow and collapsing in a heap of sadness and despair. Certainly, there were times (many times in fact) when I was overcome with moments of such grief and sadness that it overwhelmed me in that moment. But surprisingly, for much of that period, I operated on autopilot and I became the most efficient and organised that I had ever been in my life. Although I was essentially on my own, I ploughed on – slowly putting together the makings of a funeral – from planning the order of service, organising who would read on the day including the eulogy, picking the funeral plot and even the reception and the catering. The irony was not lost on me: I was organising a big church event involving Jonathan – the last time I had done so was for our wedding and now it was for Jonathan's death. How cruel fate was – but not just in respect of this but also of what emerged as I was organising the funeral.

The day started innocently enough. I was scrolling through Jonathan's mobile phone in order to contact his friends, acquaintances and colleagues to inform them of his death and of his upcoming funeral, when I came across a series of messages sent between Jonathan and another woman. A woman whom I recognised as one of his exes. The text messages themselves were not, on the face of it, highly suspicious. The messages related to an agreement to meet up during a week in February – when Jonathan was on leave around the time of his birthday. He had female friends whom he had met up with in the past. In fact there was one ex that he had remained very good friends with and whenever she was in London she would contact him to meet up and catch up with him. He had invited me to attend on a number of occasions and although I had never gone (feeling a degree of discomfort about meeting his ex and what that would entail), I had never questioned that relationship and had felt comfortable with him maintaining his friendship with her. And so when I came across this message, ordinarily I would not have paid it any mind if it weren't for one thing that bothered me – he had never told me about this meeting. From the text messages it would appear that the meeting had not in the end actually occurred – but that did not matter. It was the secrecy surrounding it which bothered me, especially combined with the fact that Jonathan was arranging to meet her at a time when I would not be around.

I felt numb and a bit sick.

I had no proof that anything suspicious had occurred. Still, the nagging feeling at the back of my mind remained.

I tried to ignore it.

I was due to register Jonathan's death and I did not want to be late. I made my way to the registry office alone. As I went up the stairs of the building, I had a flashback to the last time I was here. Jonathan and I had come to register Richard's birth, arguing about Richard's name (and his second, third and fourth name) even as we made our way out of the car and into the building. We only agreed the final order of our second child's name a few moments before we were called in. I remembered thinking that he would at least have a lot of choice if he didn't like his first name. That had made me smile back then. Now I felt nothing when revisiting the memory. As I waited in the registry office now, I kept trying to ignore the nagging feeling. *Forget about it – it's probably nothing.*

I took out Jonathan's phone. I rang the number.

The woman who answered was young. She sounded Caribbean. Jonathan's type. I broke the news of Jonathan's death bluntly – taking much less care than I normally do and listened to her shock and upset. I then lost patience and asked her straight out.

'I've seen the text messages between you and Jonathan. Did you meet up with him?'

She paused. A long pause. 'No, in the end I couldn't make it.'

This time it was me that remained silent for a while. Then I thought *what the hell.* 'Were you having an affair with him? I won't be angry. He's dead – he's gone. I just need to know. I need to know.' The weird thing was that I actually meant it. I was bone tired and weary at that point. I was about to register my husband's death. I had no energy to engage in a bitter love rival battle. The whole thing was surreal. I could only deal with one traumatic event at a time – this affair or non-affair would have to take a backseat. I just needed to know.

Her response was equivocal. A form of denial but with question marks left in the air. Perhaps not an actual affair. Yet. But certainly not an innocent friendship. My attempts to press her were unsuccessful so I asked another question. 'So why were you meeting with him?' Another long pause. I was becoming annoyed now. 'You might as well just tell me – he's gone. I just want to know!'

'He was helping me with something.'

What was this? It was like pulling teeth. 'Helping you with what?!'

'I would rather not say.'

And that was that. I was called in to register Jonathan's death and I was forced to end the call and put this to bed. My relationship with Jonathan and my grief had now reached an even higher tier on the complex level. Was I grieving a man who had been cheating on me before he died? Did I really have to contend with that as well? *Really?* As I left the registry office I knew that this was one additional strand that I absolutely could not deal with then. So as with so many things concerning Jonathan – I put it firmly to one side. I could not cope with this. *Not now. Definitely not now.*

વ્ર   વ્ર   વ્ર

Looking after two young boys and organising a funeral on my own was bad enough but as ever in my case, it was not that simple. Incredibly, I was also seriously preparing for a job interview for a legal position at a City law firm. The call for the interview had come a week or so after Jonathan's death. Although I had ceased job hunting following Jonathan's diagnosis, in the whirlwind of activity I had neglected to inform the employment agency of my circumstances. So they had continued sending out my CV to prospective law firms with the result that I had passed the initial sifting process and I had been invited to an interview – the first in a two-stage process. As soon as I saw the email I felt absurdly proud of myself, wanting to find Jonathan at once and let him know. It was moments like that – forgetting that he was gone – that often hurt the most.

I would not be sharing this news with him.

I would not be sharing any news with him ever again.

I stared at the email for a day or so not quite ready to respond. 'You can't go obviously! You've just lost your husband. You have to tell them.' My mother spoke perfect sense of course. I was a grieving widow. I had just lost my husband a week ago.

I could not carry on as though everything was OK.

But then again, why not?

One of the reasons why I was able to almost sail through the period until the funeral was because I was in denial: to me Jonathan was still there. Even as I organised his funeral – Jonathan's presence was everywhere: in the house, in our children, in my mind. I felt during that period and for many months afterwards that I was just a custodian of the house, keeping things going until he returned and this nightmare would end. The reality of the situation had not only *not* sunk in, the reality had been buried very deep underground. I could carry on and I must but only until Jonathan returned. This weird way of thinking gave me a strength that I did not know I possessed. So in addition to organising the funeral I simultaneously began preparing for an interview to the bafflement of my mother, and I hired an interview coach. I was determined to carry on living the life that I would have lived with Jonathan – in parallel with the life I was currently living in the wake of his death. This resulted in twisted and almost comical situations – such as when I went off to Westfield (by myself of course) whilst the boys were at school to shop for both a funeral outfit and a smart suit for the interview – *at the same time*. The mixed emotions of trying on outfits for a sombre awful day which would be preceded by a job interview where I would have to be upbeat and positive, selling my best self was absurd.

And insane.

The juxtaposition between my grief and my denial became jarring and exhausting. In the taxi to the interview, in a moment of terrifying honesty I started to cry and when the driver asked me why, I told him I had just lost my husband. Less than hour later however, I was before two senior partners at the law firm smiling and making small talk and answering their questions in a confident and assured manner. For the sake of one hour since Jonathan's death, it was a relief to be me – not a widow or a mother – I could pretend that I was normal, that life was normal, that nothing untoward had occurred. I felt positive and happy when I left the interview. As soon as I started to travel home however, the tears started to fall again. I had clearly made a good impression though – to my surprise and delight I was asked back for a second interview to be held several weeks later, after the funeral.

෨ ෨ ෨

Although my mind and my emotions were in a constant state of flux after Jonathan's death, a significant part of me still had to function effectively as a mother and carer. I still had to ensure that I was tending to my sons' grief and help them deal this awful period. Whilst in autopilot mode, I made use of the resources given by Charing Cross Hospital and contacted Child Bereavement UK – a charity devoted to counselling for children who were bereaved. Richard was far too young. He needed time to understand what had happened to him. On the other hand, I thought that Dominic was ready. I suppose I also felt that I needed to be doing something.

One of the things which the funeral directors had arranged was a private viewing of Jonathan's body. I had invited Jonathan's family to attend but they had declined. I cannot recall the reason they gave but it seemed that ever since Jonathan had died his family had distanced themselves from me and my sons – just watching events from afar but not joining in – in direct contrast to their presence at the hospital when Jonathan was still here. Their decision not to come was hurtful. But it did not surprise me.

Dominic was so very brave during that period. I did not think that Dominic would want to come and see his father's body either – but he did. I tried to explain to him that Jonathan would look very different and it would be a very difficult thing to do.

'I still want to see him Mummy.'

'Are you sure?'

'Yes. What will he look like?'

'He will look like Daddy except that he will be sleeping.'

Valerie stayed outside with Richard whilst Dominic and I went in to see Jonathan. We had arranged that immediately afterwards she would take the boys to buy Dominic's birthday present – the goldfish he wanted – therefore ending the visit with an uplifting trip to bring a new addition to the house. Dominic and I were led down a corridor into a room. It was dimly lit and very cool. Jonathan lay there. It was not quite Jonathan – his face was different – it had taken on a grey shade. His features were more elongated in some ways. It was eerie looking at him. I tried to shield Dominic initially. However, he was determined to see him. I fought against my instincts to stop him and allowed myself to be led by him. He was young yes, but he was also at that age when he knew his own mind. This may be a way for him to eventually gain closure I thought. He cried silently and I held him. When he left, he was quiet but calm. I believed then that that was the right decision – it was clearly something he felt he needed to do at that time.

    ⁀   ⁀   ⁀

One issue that became more pressing in the immediate aftermath of Jonathan's death was the delicate matter of my finances. Jonathan and I had never discussed the financial aspects of any death in service whilst he was working for the NHS. And of course, his preoccupation with his research project took precedence over discussing with me the financial implications of his death. I don't believe I was angry with him then about this, certainly not while he was in the hospital, but as time passed I felt a quiet fury towards him.

  Jonathan's research project had played such a huge part of his life and was without a doubt one of the most important things in his life. For some time after his death, particularly on those occasions when I would be struggling to make sense of the financial situation I was in and trying to figure out what came next, I felt an overwhelming sense of anger and resentment towards Jonathan. It seemed to me that in his last dying days, instead of prioritising how to ensure that I and the children were taken care of, to ensure that I had access to all the financial papers that I needed, to ensure that the children and I would not be left floundering when he was finally gone, instead of putting us first – he had once again put his project first. So that of course when he passed away, I was in the precarious position of having very little in the way of immediate funds. He had been too busy protecting one of his most important legacies – his research project. That fury has over time abated somewhat as I realise that whether he intended to or not, Jonathan had left me in a decent position. I had a house, and some money for me and the children that could deal with pressing financial issues – we would be protected – for now at least.

Interestingly, the whole experience concerning my financial circumstances did also do something else other than highlight my frustration with Jonathan – it opened up a new door into Jonathan's world. In particular, I was humbled by the HR team at Jonathan's hospital who reached out to me very early on after Jonathan's death. They wanted to help me sort out the financial paperwork which needed to be dealt with following his death. I was so thankful to the lovely lady in HR who bristled with efficiency and sympathy whilst obtaining my signature to the various forms she completed with speed.

It was an odd experience going into Jonathan's workplace. This was Jonathan's world – a world I had heard much about it but which I had never really visited save for the odd Christmas dinner or social event. As I was treated with care and kindness whilst taken through the floor to the HR office, I could see that Jonathan had been revered and certainly in some quarters really loved. I struggled with this on so many levels. The Jonathan I had known had been at times so difficult to be with, to live with, to be close to and to maintain a harmonious relationship. But amongst his colleagues he had clearly shown a consistently compassionate side – at the very least a side that lent itself to so much good will and genuine remorse from his colleagues. I had witnessed this with David's open display of emotion when we had spoken on the phone just before Jonathan had died. So too with the colleagues who had come to the hospital to see him. I shouldn't have been surprised then when David reached out to me shortly before the funeral to ask if he and a few colleagues could come to the house to see me.

'I'm not sure I can – I am so busy with everything including the funeral arrangements.'

'Please – some colleagues would like to just come and pay their respects and show their support.'

'Really David I am not sure that I can handle that, not right now.'

'Please Thelma, we are all broken up about Jonathan's death and we all just want to support you.'

I relented. David was insistent and I was tired. I did not have the energy to wave him off. Besides which I did understand – I was still in shock but I had had the benefit of knowing for three weeks. They had known of his illness only a few days before he died. When they came however, it became apparent that things were not quite as David had made out. The first thing was the number of people who arrived by far surpassing the 'few' colleagues that he had referred to in our conversation. I recall having to scramble for extra chairs as they had taken all the seats in the living room. The second was that as supportive as they may have wanted to be, the atmosphere I sensed was also ringed with annoyance.

'Why weren't we told? We didn't know!' One of the nurses spoke up – her tone laced with frustration. I had no idea if that frustration was directed at me or Jonathan. Either way, I felt decidedly defensive.

'It all happened so fast. He was only diagnosed a few weeks before he died. The boys and I are in shock too.'

I imagine it must have been extremely hard for them – to lose a colleague that they valued so much in such an abrupt fashion – with no warning, just a leave of absence from work and then death. It was fortuitous that they had come however – I did not know it then but I really, really needed them. As efficient as I thought I had been in sorting out the funeral arrangements there were many gaps that I had not filled and some that I had not even thought of. It had been extremely hard juggling funeral arrangements on my own, whilst also looking after two very young children. And oh yes, not to mention the small matter of preparing for an interview.

I could feel their eyes on me as I drank my tea. They asked me about the funeral arrangements, with the same outspoken nurse querying:

'Are you doing all this on your own? Where are the family members to help?'

Indeed – where were they? In that moment I felt almost ashamed. And so very alone.

I cannot remember how I responded to this question. But it did not matter. In that instant, everything changed. From the outside, they must have seen the huge undertaking I was trying to work through, even though I could not see it myself at the time. They insisted on helping with the practicalities of the funeral – such as ushering, bringing the photos of Jonathan to the church, helping with all sorts of things that I had not thought of and which frankly, had I thought of it doubt that I would have been able to do. David was responsible for contacting all of Jonathan's patients. Jonathan had given instructions that all patients who wanted to come should come to the funeral. David had tried to explain to me how daunting this task was as the patient list exceeded hundreds. I remember being initially unsympathetic to his suggestions that this figure should be trimmed down. In the end it was agreed that it would be sensible to allow those who could come at short notice to attend this funeral and then organise another service in the new year for all those unable to make it now. This seemed like a fair compromise.

The way that Jonathan's colleagues had rallied round to help me was in direct contrast to both Jonathan's family and my own. Even though they were my kin and could see the awful position I was in, my own family did not do a great deal to help me. My sister as usual, retreated into the background unable to offer any real assistance. She was certainly pretty upset and devastated by the death of Jonathan. However, that level of emotion was no good to me when I needed help with the practical things of organising a funeral. In addition, apart from accompanying me to the funeral parlour for the initial appointment in selecting caskets and cemetery plots – my mother had not provided any more practical help, although she offered moral support. Jonathan's family on the other hand disappeared. I did not see Tom, I did not see June nor Patricia and Vincent at all during the period I was organising the funeral.

My mother saw what was going on and kept saying, 'You cannot do this all by yourself – you need help!' Well that was easier said than done. Apart from Jonathan's colleagues who had now volunteered to help with the mechanics of the day, from whom was I going to receive this mystery help? I chose to ignore my mother whenever she said this – not wanting to expend my energy explaining the inexplicable.

My mother was unconvinced by my reaction – she decided that she must try to get help for me. She contacted Patricia and must have put the case to her that I needed assistance with the funeral arrangements, especially from Tom as he was Jonathan's brother. However, it was not Tom who made contact with me – but June. When I heard the familiar ping of a new text message on my phone I expected it to be my mother – I was surprised to see the message from my sister-in-law. It was a brief one liner stating that I should let her know if I needed help with the funeral arrangements and that she was thinking of me.

It was a friendly helpful message on the face of it. It disturbed me at the time that Tom was not included in that text, implying that he did not want much to do with the funeral arrangements of his brother. Even so, here finally was a clear offer of help from Jonathan's family. And God knows, I really could have done with some help at that time – it would have lightened the huge load on my shoulders.

And yet.

I was deeply uncomfortable with June's text. Aside from the fact that I did not know her very well, when reading her text I had flashbacks of her over the past few weeks – the accusing tone to me when I had brought Jonathan to see his family after the cancer diagnosis, the way that she had spoken to me and had made me feel (whether she intended to or not) as though Jonathan's deterioration was my fault for not seeing it. And, of course, the raising of her eyebrows and disapproval when I said that I needed money to start the funeral arrangements.

Rightly or wrongly, my strong gut and instinct was that this was not a person whom would be fully supportive. I did not trust her and her lack of real warmth towards me meant that I was not comfortable having her by my side at my most vulnerable. So after much deliberation, knowing I could regret my decision in the future, I replied with a brief thank you and put her and her text to one side. I would carry on alone.

My exchanges with the rest of the in-laws, particularly between me and Patricia, were initially polite and mutually supportive, recognising in each other the need to keep going even whilst grieving. Patricia sent me a few texts confirming that she was ready to help if I needed anything from her (I didn't believe it but acknowledged it). She also asked me to tell her what had been organised so far and I duly replied – giving her the updates that she required without a second thought. I was still in efficiency mode, my first priority being to organise the funeral, a task which was all consuming.

Patricia did appear to notice how organised I was, commenting in one of her texts that I 'seem on top of things.' It was certainly nice that Patricia had acknowledged just how efficient I was. However, as the funeral arrangements gained pace and reached a more advanced stage, I became increasingly constrained by lack of funds. It is a strange experience to be planning for a funeral with a reception costing thousands of pounds but not actually have the money in place for any of it to go ahead. Shortly after the initial texts with her I had a phone call with Patricia whereupon I updated her on the plans so far particularly regarding the church service and the readings to be carried out and so on. My mother was in the room when I had this conversation with Patricia. After we finished speaking, my no-nonsense Nigerian mother said, 'Why has she not mentioned money?'

'She already said that she would pay for it when she was here, the day after Jonathan died.'

'But she has not said it since – not once in that conversation with you just now did Patricia mention that she would pay for it!'

I admit that without my mother's presence I probably would not have thought it was a big deal. My mother is often prone to paranoid thoughts about others. But in this she was right. In a way. I needed more than an assurance made a few weeks ago – I needed the actual funds now. In this more assertive frame of mind, I crafted a text to Patricia setting out very clearly why I needed her to make good on her promise now. Patricia's response was immediate and curt, saying that she had made it clear to me that she would 'tide me over' during this period and that she had posted a cheque to me earlier that evening. She added that she had found my text 'upsetting.'

'Just ignore it,' my mother said in response to the text from Patricia. Nonetheless I could not help feeling guilty – perhaps I (and my mother) had read the situation wrong. However, no matter – Patricia had confirmed that she had posted the cheque and that was all that mattered. I carried on busying myself with the funeral arrangements. A few days later, I received a zinger of a text from Patricia which made me furious. The text started off well enough praising my efforts and saying that I had 'done an excellent job in organising the funeral'. After confirming that she was working with Tom on his eulogy she said that they had wondered if I would create a new 'photographic display' on a headboard for the church. This headboard would be in addition to any other photos I would be bringing to the church. She added that they could '*email loads of photos for you to choose from and I think this task would be especially helpful for Dominic and Richard.'*

In retrospect, perhaps I overreacted to the request to make a headboard. This kind of mindful activity probably has its place sometime after the death of a loved one.

But.

I was busy and exhausted from rushing around trying to piece together the itinerary for Jonathan's funeral. I was busy from looking after two young children under the age of eight. I was busy from preparing for an interview for a job I might well desperately need, certainly until my financial position became clear. So when Patricia sent me a text giving me yet another task to do on top of the *many* others that I was wading through, I saw red. In many ways my reaction was irrational and unfair – after all June had offered to help me – help which I had firmly refused.

Even so, I could not help the resentment which rose to the surface. From the comfort of their countryside Aga kitchen, it seemed that my in-laws were calmly dictating to me what I should be doing whilst I was rushing around in a whirlwind of stress and anxiety. My response was sharp but veiled with politeness:

'*The cheque for the funeral has arrived, thank you. As soon as it clears my account I will forward the full amount to the funeral arrangers so Jonathan's funeral can go ahead. Concerning the photographic display that sounds like a good idea. However, I am pretty inundated at the moment with the funeral arrangements as it currently stands which I am still wading through, looking after the boys and managing Dominic's grief, all of which I am doing largely on my own so I do not have the capacity to take on any additional tasks. Perhaps this is something you could ask Tom or one of his three children to do? (who are more likely to be more technologically minded anyway!)... Tx'*

I did not receive an immediate response to my blunt text but neither was I expecting to. I hoped that silence would now prevail until the funeral itself.

I was wrong.

A day or so later I received a text from her confirming that June and her daughter would do the photo collage. She also said that Tom and June were helping her and Vincent get through this time and that *'we trust that you are getting similar support from your mother and sister and are not carrying too much on your own'.*

I had now reached the point with Patricia that I dreaded her texts. It seemed that every few days there would be something. I decided to try and put her on mute in order to get to the end stage of the funeral preparation. I just needed to be left in peace. No such luck though: I received another text from her shortly afterwards concerning the sending of birthday presents to Dominic before the funeral and updating me on the work she and her family had been doing on the eulogy and the photo storyboard. She ended by stating again that Tom and June had been a 'wonderful support' to her and Vincent.

That last sentence made me a stop for a while. I was overcome momentarily with rage and jealousy. I felt like screaming at the text *'at least you have wonderful support – I have no one!'*

I overcame my urge to respond.

Just ignore it I told myself – she will get bored and stop. She will. Any minute now.

No such luck. I received another text from Patricia. It began with a slight rebuke stating that she had hoped I would reply to her by now. She asked after the boys, wanting confirmation that Dominic had received his birthday presents and wondering how Richard was reacting to all that had happened. She again said in the text that she and her family were very willing to help and I just needed 'to ask.' And again the inclusion of the sentence that irked me so much '*I trust you are finding the support you need in the company of your mother and sister.*'

Her insistence in constantly referring to the 'support' I must be receiving from my mother and sister was repetitive.

And deeply annoying.

I felt obliged to set her straight.

'*Hi [Patricia] ... whereas the emotional support from my mother and sister is there, for various reasons they are not able to provide practical support. So as I have said in my earlier text to you, I am largely on my own concerning funeral arrangements, caring for the boys etc. ... However, the funeral arrangements are at its end stages now. I am reviewing the draft Order of Service and will send out soft copies to all relevant people before funeral. The ushers etc have been organised etc. ... so I am pretty much there now. T.*'

This last text I sent marked the end of the civil relations between us. Her next text to me essentially provoked me.

The war then officially started.

Her text to me got straight to the point. She had 'decided' that she and Vincent would come to London the day before the funeral. They would stay overnight in a hotel and then come to my house early in the morning. Tom and June would follow, arriving at my house later that morning. She would be bringing a wheelchair for Vincent and requested that I make sure they were seated right in front of the speakers and that they were close to amenities.

It was an innocuous text on the face of it. However, the presumptuous nature of it (rightly or wrongly) tipped me over the edge. Perhaps it was her request that I should ensure that she and Vincent are seated in the best places for them. Or maybe it was the way she began the text with no greeting – no preamble – just straight into informing me what she was doing and wanting to ensure that I complied with her needs. I felt like some sort of servant – rushing around to organise a funeral for her son whilst she sat at home and now that it was close to the funeral she would swoop down to make her presence felt. It brought home to me just how much I had taken on my shoulders. I began to seethe with resentment and rage. I decided there and then that the funeral day would be as comfortable as it could be for me and the boys. That meant that I wanted to minimise contact with her and her family. The thought of having them in the house, turning their noses up whilst I would run around making tea for them, trying to be a good host whilst also trying to coordinate the funeral on my own was all too much to bear. That would be it.

'I don't want them in my house.'

My mother laughed at my words. We were in my living room watching the boys play with their toys at our feet. She stopped when she saw the serious look on my face. She said slowly, 'You can't do that.'

'Oh yes, I can. I don't want them here. I do not want them in my house.'

I am not proud of myself.

I contrived a pretext based on Dominic's counselling (where he had actually expressed reservations about having a house full of people on the day of the funeral) as the reason why they should not come here. I was sure that Patricia would see through it. But I was desperate. I did not want them here. It was time to let her know.

'[Patricia], there are few things I need to let you know and was going to tell you next week but this seems like the best time to do it given your text. I have spoken recently with the child bereavement counsellor and been speaking with [Dominic] at length about the funeral over the past few days. He wants and needs to come but understandably it is causing him a great deal of turmoil. The counsellor and I have agreed with him that our house will be a 'sanctuary', 'a people free zone' both before and after the funeral. So apart from myself and my mother and my sister who will help me look after the kids and who will be here already no one else will be in the house all day so he can be alone with those he is most closest to in the house before the funeral and avoid the stress of a teeming house. He struggles now when people come to the house to talk about Jonathan and we need to avoid any excess stress for him on the day. By ensuring this he can also return any time he likes to the house knowing it will be safe, comforting and not filled with people. So you, [Vincent] et al should aim to arrive just before 10.30 am outside the house so you can all go straight from your cars into the limousine without needing to come inside the house. I know this may be difficult for you all but [I] have promised [Dominic] this and his welfare and mental health during this distressing period is my first priority. Concerning the church, I am sure you and Tom can ask Charles [the church priest] where the best seating arrangements will be for you

when you arrive – Charles will be the best person to know.
The church has toilets immediately in front of you when you
arrive. I don't know about the cemetery, but that again I am
sure you can find out with the help of Tom and June when
you arrive there. Tom and June's primary purpose will be to
look after you and Vincent all day I am sure, as my primary
purpose is to look after my children on this difficult day and I
am sure you can ask them to do all these things for you then. T.'

The energy it took to write the email was all consuming but I
welcomed it.

I felt bullish. And sated.

The knives came out. Patricia was not happy at all with
this as she soon made clear. I could feel her anger emanating
from the text. She responded, '*Vincent and I are Dominic and*
Richard's grandparents and do not consider they will be distressed
if we arrive in good time for the funeral and spend a little time in the
house with you.' She ended the text firmly with '*We do not wish*
to be denied access to the house. The idea is monstrous.'

But I was too far gone. The more she tried to argue with
me the more furious I became. And all the resentment and
anger I had towards her and Tom came to the fore. I dug in
even deeper:

'*Patricia. You and Tom came to my house a few weeks ago,*
after declaring that it was a "mess" then proceeded to go
through my things, in my personal bedroom, without my
consent. You did this because you thought you were acting
in the interests of Jonathan. I found it incredibly distressing
that you and Tom could violate my privacy in this way. But
you did it nevertheless. You will say that you believed you
were acting in Jonathan's best interests so I let it go. Well

now we are in a position where my son, your grandson, has lost his father forever in a matter of 3 weeks. Have you even considered the psychological harm that he (and Richard) will now go through? If there is anything I can do to alleviate the stress of a 7 year old boy burying his father then I WILL DO IT. You will arrive before 10.30 am and you will not attempt to make a scene or make a difficult day any worse. This [is] about [Dominic]. Not you.'

Her text was immediate and scathing. She said that Jonathan had instructed them to clear his bedroom and she thought that she and Tom were helping both of us. She ended with *'We will arrive when we arrive and do not expect to be denied access to the house and left standing on the pavement.'* I responded in kind:

'That is precisely what will happen Patricia. I made a promise to my son and I will keep it. That is the end of this conversation as far as I'm concerned.'

Patricia's response was more contrite. She said that she expected to be treated with 'kindness and courtesy', that she had lost her son like Dominic had lost his father and she hoped that 'we can all find comfort in each other's company', adding that Tom and June felt the same. She ended by saying, *'We all want the children to grow up loved and cherished by their family.'*

I was not moved by this text such was my anger and exhaustion at the time. At this point I had no idea whether Patricia would turn up at my door demanding access or whether she would accept the situation. All I knew was that I felt for the first time like I was actually in control of the situation and was exercising my right to do what felt right for me – not Jonathan, not Patricia not Vincent and not Tom – but me. Well there was only one way to find out if Patricia would heed my warning. The day of the funeral was now imminent – creating a ball of dread inside my stomach which began to gradually unravel as the day drew near.

CHAPTER 7

The Funeral

*A*s Jonathan's funeral day arrived, I realised that whereas I had seen many funerals on TV, in movies or described in books, I had actually only ever attended one in real life – my father's funeral. His funeral had occurred four years earlier. I had been estranged from my father for many years by the time he died, and that, combined with the fact that I was recovering from one of my miscarriages meant that the organisation for the funeral had been left to my mother. I had no part in it and had deliberately detached myself from the whole process. I had attended on the day however, full of emotion and tears – crying for the father I had lost many years before – not the one that was in a casket a mere few metres away. And now here I was attending another. One that I would be playing an instrumental role in.

I was not looking forward to this.

It is the strangest thing getting ready for a funeral. On what must be one of the saddest days of my life I still had to put my best foot forward. I woke up with the ball of dread still in my stomach – it had not shifted overnight – sleep had only bought me a brief respite. As I brought out the black outfit that I had recently bought and placed it on my bed I suddenly felt so tired already. *Please let this be over with soon.* I took care with my make-up, trying to look good but not *too good* (lest people think that I was not sad enough). The boys also needed to look their best and I took the time to get them dressed carefully in sombre clothing that would suit the occasion.

In the end, when the in-laws arrived, we were all polite and cordial. The day, with all the guests, amounting to over 100 (including the former patients of Jonathan who were able to attend), would be a big one, with all eyes on us. The day was about Jonathan first and foremost. So there was no scene outside the house. We got ready and entered the cars lined up on the pavement waiting for us.

True to their word, those of Jonathan's colleagues who had volunteered to help with so much of the funeral logistics had turned up and were dutifully carrying out their agreed roles – acting as usher, helping to direct people with the parking, bringing the photos of Jonathan for the viewing and generally being the help that I did not know that I actually needed until they came to visit me. I was touched too by the kindness of the two parent mums who actually came to the funeral – Kathy and Lucy. Kathy had brought her son Peter as well, which was a lovely thing to do – he was a close friend of Dominic and him being there helped to make the day so much more palatable for him.

The commencement of the funeral brought with it feelings of being disconnected. When I arrived initially I was greeted by a sea of faces. Apart from Jonathan's colleagues, I did not recognise many at first. These must be Jonathan's patients. Eventually as I moved down the aisle to the front, I began to recognise others from my husband's life. His close friends from his days as a medical student at London university were present: Victoria and Faye, present with their families – the tears already present even before they saw me. It was a relief to actually see people that I knew and had met before and I hugged them closely feeling that connection to Jonathan.

This was the exact converse of our wedding – a church event I had also organised and which had started by my seeing and greeting Jonathan's old friends – except that on this occasion every hug, every handshake, every kiss on the cheek was accompanied by tears and a heavy sorrowful heart. And also with the feeling that this was all so very wrong – we should not be here, this was not supposed to happen.

As I made my way further up the aisle to where I would be sitting with the children, Charles, the priest, beckoned me over even as the guests were still arriving.

'Would any of the family members like to be pallbearers?'

'What do you mean?'

'The funeral directors can carry the body but often some family members – normally the males in the family like to carry the coffin.'

'I don't know. I will ask.'

I placed my bags down and made my way to the front of the church where Patricia, Vincent, Tom and his family were all sitting. I asked Tom if he and his sons would like to carry Jonathan's coffin. I genuinely expected that they would. After all this was their relative, their flesh and blood.

I saw Tom ask the question of his two sons, Jonathan's nephews – both in their thirties by now but for some reason looking much younger in the church lighting. I saw his sons shake their heads one by one: they did not want to carry Jonathan's coffin. Any disappointment I may have felt I immediately stamped out – I needed to put it to one side for now: I still had to get through the funeral. If only this was the worst thing that could have happened at the service. Unfortunately, there was more to come.

The ceremony was awful in many respects. The 'family' sat at the front – all in a row. Their backs to the congregation, their backs to me. Rigid and distant. A family turned in on itself and whose dislike for me was clear. I, and my sons, my mother and sister sat a few rows back. The clear division between us all evident to see – we were separated – not only physically but also in so many other ways. The rage and anger I felt that day was pushed down and subdued. To be examined and dealt with at a later date. *Not now, just get through the day.*

Dominic was stoic in the church – on the verge of tears but surprisingly calm. Richard, on the other hand, was not. He cried during the ceremony, at times openly asking 'Where is Daddy?', his voice cutting across the church hall and causing all those who heard it to momentarily freeze before the inevitable mutterings could be heard. I did not know how to deal with this. It was a heartbreaking thing to hear from your youngest when burying your husband, their father. I held him close. But even as the tears fell I continued to face forward and willed the ceremony to continue.

Even amongst the painful aspects of the ceremony, there were some beautiful moments during that church service. Church readings were done by his work colleagues and friends, in particular Michael and Amaka, the two colleagues who had visited Jonathan in hospital and had tearfully pleaded to see him one last time. There were tributes too from people from different areas of Jonathan's life – his university friend Victoria, his running friend Edward from the local running club and one from his longstanding patient – Paul. There was also a lovely solo piece of *Pie Jesu* by Gabriel Fauré sung by Victoria's daughter, Bella. For a moment, as I heard the wonderful tributes to Jonathan I experienced a ray of sunshine – of hope during the ceremony. *It's not that bad. I can do this. I can get through this.*

And then it was Tom's turn to do his eulogy. The clouds descended again.

As Tom went to the front of the church to deliver the eulogy, the familiar ball of dread in my stomach hardened. I closed my eyes as he began to speak. This was a eulogy that spoke of Jonathan as a child and as a man; as Tom's brother and as an uncle to his children. The eulogy, was also very distinctive in another way: although I had been married to Jonathan for almost 10 years, and we had two children together, whom Jonathan had loved very much – Tom's eulogy had only one sentence that mentioned me and our children – right at the end along the lines of: 'He then met Thelma and they got married and had Dominic and Richard.' That was it.

Is that it?

Is that it?

There was no outlet – I was still at the funeral – all eyes were still on me and on my children. I kept the mask on and hoped my face showed little emotion.

But I was furious underneath.

My role in Jonathan's life was dismissed to be of so little importance as to take up no more than several words in a eulogy. I felt in that moment that the family truly were the most abhorrent human beings I had ever come across in my life. I thought of all the efforts that I had made in organising the funeral by myself, picking out the readings, the photos, the order of service – all without the help of the family who had effectively swanned in, sat in the front row and then denigrated me in front of the congregation. The rage and the anger had to be suppressed. I would still need to get through the day. *Not now, not now.*

There was a beautiful reading of a poem that I had picked for the service which was read by Faye, Jonathan's other good friend from university. A wonderful piece by David Harkins called 'Remember Me'. I listened to the words with pride. I felt that the words of that poem summed up Jonathan very well – talking of how he would have wanted to be remembered by those he had left behind. The last sentence in particular really resonated with me: '*You can cry and close your mind, Be empty and turn your back, Or you can do what he would want, Smile, open your eyes, love and go on.*'

In that moment, as the ceremony came to a close, I suddenly felt proud of myself – not because of the organisation of the service but for actually getting through it. I had done it. *It's over, thank God it's over.*

☙   ☙   ☙

It was over.

It was finally done.

I don't know why but despite everything, including my intense anger towards Jonathan's family, I still felt a need to reach out to Patricia. Perhaps it was the feeling of emptiness that accompanied me at the end of the service, the feeling that I was completely depleted, after I had poured so much energy into it. Or perhaps it was because I felt a need to connect with Jonathan on some level - and in his absence his family members, notwithstanding the pain they had caused, were still the nearest thing to him.

People had now began clearing their things and preparing to go to the cemetery. Patricia was wheeling Vincent towards the exit. As I passed her I said: 'I found all this really hard – it was tough to do things like pick out the coffin for him. Really hard.'

Patricia did not quite look at me. 'I still have all this to come with Vincent.' Her tone was flat. She turned back to Vincent. That was it.

No acknowledgement about her son's funeral, about the task that her daughter-in-law had undertaken largely on her own. Instead, her response was framed in such a way so as to refer to her – her future suffering. There was to be no thank you for me.

It was raining by the time we arrived at the cemetery. The ground at Willesden Cemetery was wet and incredibly muddy. I had never come to this cemetery before. It was not an experience that I was looking forward to.

As we walked to the burial site, the emotional see-saw that I was riding on veered over dangerously to one side. This was becoming so very real now. On some unconscious level, although he had yet to process the death of his father and the full implications of that, Richard must have realised that something was going on. His restlessness in church became more pronounced at the graveyard. It was clear that he could not be there at that time. Valerie and her other nanny friends kindly stepped in at this point and took Richard away for a walk whilst his father was being buried. In essence, they acted as the practical support with the boys that I needed on the day – the kind of practical support that had been completely absent from Jonathan's family. Also the kind of support which in fairness had also been absent from my own mother and sister. Yes my mother was there in the form of emotional support, but my sister was as usual present in body only and more than a little distant, even as it was obvious that she was undergoing her own grief.

The service at the side of the grave was mercifully brief. I don't remember what was said by Charles as he carried out the funeral rites in the rain. I only remember standing with Dominic beside me, both of us crying silently, our heads bowed. At some point there was silence. Dominic and I threw a rose onto the coffin although I cannot recall how we came to have the flowers or who had given them to us. We stared at the coffin adorned on the top with two intertwined roses. Dominic and I remained rooted to the spot. Just earlier this morning, before the day had even started, I had wanted it to end. And now I wanted this moment to continue forever. *This is not happening.*

This is not happening.

We could not move.

Jonathan was in the ground.

He was gone.

Really. Gone.

At that moment nothing made any sense to me. A part of my life, one half of my partnership, the father of my children was dead, soon to be buried and I could not physically move. I wished then, and many times since that I could stay by Jonathan's side. That I could remain at the graveside immobile and passive for an eternity. But, this could not be done today. Dominic and I had to go. It was Tom who gently took us away from the side – one act of genuine kindness from him that day.

The reception was held at a local pub on the Harrow Road, very near to our home and to the church. It was a fitting place in many ways as it was very near to Notting Hill, an area of London that had held such fond memories for Jonathan, as he had told me on many occasions. It was also a pub that Jonathan had pointed out to me once and had said that he always wanted to try. It seemed right that it should be the venue for his reception.

It was a quiet establishment with a pleasant spacious decor punctuated with oak panelling in the manner of most traditional pubs. It had a pretty little patioed beer garden as well. And that was the first place I went to as soon as I arrived and as the other guests started trooping in.

I could not breathe.

I was tearful and empty inside. I just wanted to go home.

'Are you all right?'

My mother had followed me outside.

'I don't think I can do it.'

The 'it' clearly needed no explanation. My mother put her arm round me.

'You are doing so well. You can do this. You are strong. You can do this.' I leaned into her hug but said nothing.

It was the final act of a three part farewell to Jonathan – the church service and the burial were done – the last part now remained: the reception. I went back inside and the room had filled up. People had taken various seats at the tables spread out. Patricia and her family had arrived and they now stood in the middle of the room. Patricia stood with her back rigid and straight, not quite looking at me but clearly aware of my presence. In that instant I was filled with the anger and rage that was fast becoming my constant companion. I knew why she was standing like that – refusing to do as others had done around her – namely find a table and then take a seat. She was standing there expecting someone, no doubt me, to find her a table, to treat her and her family as the important guests. It was reminiscent of her behaviour at my wedding – expecting to take centre stage. My anger and stubbornness rose to the fore. This was not her day – this was about Jonathan. So I ignored her. I went and spoke to Jonathan's friends and others. I forced myself to mingle – to talk and to remember

Jonathan. It felt false and unnatural and many viewed me, or so I thought, with a mixture of pity and bemusement. But I did it anyway.

From the corner of my eye, I saw that Jonathan's family eventually settled on a table in the middle of the room. And as with the church service they stayed apart from the others.

'It was a good service wasn't it?'

Tom was eating. He held a plate with food in one hand, the other hand picking at the finger food he had selected from the piles of trays. I had not noticed him come to stand next to me by the buffet table.

'Yes it was.' I could barely look at him. He had done a eulogy that had barely mentioned me, that had been insulting to me and yet here he was trying to make casual conversation with me as though nothing had happened. I wanted to scream at him at that moment.

'That priest, Charles is it? He was really good.'

'Sorry, will you excuse me?' I had to leave him. I could not bear to be in his presence any longer.

I went to check in on Dominic. He was with his friend Peter and surprisingly, he was in fine spirits. It was odd to see him laughing and having fun with his friend. I imagine that grief for a child is an unbearable weight on young shoulders and any moment of light relief should be seized. I gave him a hug holding him tightly against my chest, blinking away my tears. I savoured the moment with him for a little while longer before I left him with his friend and continued to mingle.

Eventually I ran out of steam. The pub began to thin out. I was tapped on the shoulder and I turned. It was Patricia.

'Vincent wants a word with you.'

I went to Vincent and knelt by his wheelchair. Just as at my house, of all the family members, Vincent was the only one who seemed to have any genuine emotion regarding the loss of Jonathan. He was also the only person who did not seem to be filled with outright hostility towards to me.

'Oh Thelma, I am so very sorry, I am so, so sorry.' Vincent cried, his thin fragile frame shaking as tears coursed down his cheeks. I hugged him and kissed his head, crying too. I felt bonded to him in that moment in a way that I had never really bonded before. I stayed with him a few moments then gave him one final hug goodbye before I moved away. This time my tears were clearly visible.

The 'family' left shortly afterwards. I assisted in calling them a taxi so they could pick up their cars from my street and leave. With the exception of Vincent I was glad to see them go. They made me feel uncomfortable and so deeply unhappy. I went back to the reception and then eventually left with my mother and sister, Valerie and the boys. I was so relieved to be home again. I imagined that all would be calm from here onwards and I could now focus on myself and my boys.

If only.

CHAPTER 8

The Fury

'Everyone wants to help but they don't know what to do.' Lucy said this with some frustration. We were outside the school gates at this point on one of the many days or weeks after the funeral – I couldn't be sure which – time had passed by in a chaotic blur since the funeral. I have to confess that I had not really noticed that much how the parents had stayed away until much later. Such was my detachment from the parent body.

But Lucy was right.

After the funeral, just as they had done immediately after Jonathan's death, the majority of the other parents had largely stayed away. I could be kind and say that they did not know what to say to me and that this awkwardness prevented them from having any kind of dialogue with me. If I were being truthful I would say that my apparent 'resilience' probably repelled them. They simply did not know what to do with it or how to respond to it. So it was easier to just stay away.

And of course gossip from afar.

All understandable.

Maybe.

But Lucy's statement still annoyed me intensely at the time. The implication seemed to be that it was my fault – in other words, why could I not make myself more accessible so that they could help out more and feel useful? It seems incredulous now that what may have been obvious to an outside observer was not apparent to them – that I was clearly in shock and therefore would have been unlikely to be acting or thinking normally. Perhaps my self-sufficiency was such that it thwarted or prevented others (with the exception of the likes of Kathy and Lucy) from doing the natural thing – which is to take control, gently insist on taking over tasks and just actually helping. Then again, it seems unfair to criticise them unduly. After all there is no manual on how to deal with grief and there is no manual on how to help those dealing with intense grief. So despite my disappointment with Lucy's comments I set it to one side.

To be honest, much of what went on with the parent body I was oblivious to during this period. My attention in the immediate aftermath of the funeral was again taken up with the in-laws. My brief time with Vincent after the funeral stayed with me long afterwards. When I woke the next day after the funeral I felt very strongly that I must reach out to him – the only member of Jonathan's family who had showed me some kindness on the day that I had buried his son. I decided that I should write to him – my way of thanking him for making a very difficult day just that little bit easier by his compassion and care for me in that one moment. However, Vincent did not have a direct email address and even if he did, he left all matters of correspondence to Patricia. If I wanted to communicate with him then I would need to do so through his wife. The idea of doing this did not fill me with joy but I had little choice – the email to her husband was sent directly to her – which meant that I had to be careful of its contents.

However, I had no intention of curtailing what I needed to say.

'Patricia, this email is for Vincent. Could you please print off for him to read or read it to him please – whichever is easiest.

Dear Vincent,

I woke up today after the funeral of Jonathan and guess who I was thinking of? I was thinking of you. You were on my mind because your kind words to me moved me to tears. You said 'I missed you' and I felt in those words your genuine heartfelt compassion for me and the boys. I saw the pain and grief in your eyes and I believe when you looked at me you would have seen the same. In that connection I felt very close to you and very close to the memory of Jonathan. You are a genuine and lovely man. Bless you Vincent.

We did not get much time to talk as you were leaving but there are two things I would like to do for you to try and help you in this devastating situation that we and the boys find ourselves in.

The first is I would like to refer you again to the Order of Service. I am sure you will have taken a hard copy of it from yesterday but just in case I have attached a soft copy to this email. You see I selected all the hymns and the readings for the Order of Service and organised for [Bella] to sing as a soprano. But concerning the 2 readings in particular I struggled initially. I found the Lamentations scripture first and when I tried to find another scripture reading to complement it I found that extremely hard. Just by chance I happened to look at the non-scripture readings that Charles the priest had given me and I decided to have a quick flick through (thinking I would still prefer another reading from the Bible). However, I came across the poem by David Harkins, 'Remember Me' and after reading it, I was in tears. I knew this was the one. I specifically asked the printers to include this reading in the Order of Service printed out (normally they only include the

*hymns not the readings). I wanted it there because I wanted
people to take comfort from it, even after the funeral. And now
I commend this to you. Please read the poem regularly. I read
it quite frequently now. I find that it gives me just a little bit
of peace during this terrible time.*

*The second thing is that I would like to give you a gift. You
may recall at the funeral service in church that there was a
lovely large framed photo of Jonathan at work. He is smiling
and looking happy and relaxed. I am getting a framed copy
made and I would like to give that copy to you. Whenever I
see that photo it makes me sad and happy at the same time.
However, I take heart from the fact that at the time it was taken
Jonathan was happy and healthy – the way we would want to
remember him. I will send it to you hopefully by the end of
next week. You should receive it in the next couple of weeks.*

*That's it for now. I am extremely tired now and the grief is
finally catching up with me having kept it at bay for the past
few weeks in order to organise the funeral.*

*If you like, I would like to write to you again, when I am
feeling stronger.*

All my love, Thelma.'

I know that it would have irked Patricia for me to send
an email direct to her husband and ignore her entirely –
effectively treating her as no more than a conduit to Vincent.
However, I did not want to engage with her or communicate
with her in any meaningful way. Not then. I simply did
not have the time or energy for her. After I sent the email,
mentally I felt a bit lighter as though a small load had been
lifted off my shoulders. That feeling did not last long: a few
days later I received an email from Patricia.

She started off by thanking me on behalf of Vincent for his gift of Jonathan's photograph. She referred to the grief and loss that she and Vincent were struggling with, along with the grief that I must be enduring but points out that I do have the children who will now be the main focus of my life. She continued by inviting me and the boys to come and stay with her and Vincent so we could all visit the theatre and watch a pantomime that she had previously booked for all of us (including Jonathan). This had been one of the things that she would always do for us whenever we came down at Christmastime to visit her and Vincent – book interesting events and shows for all of us to attend. Dominic and Richard always used to enjoy that so much. I thought about it and for a moment I was tempted to seriously consider coming – for old times' sake.

But then I read the rest of her email and saw the bomb that she had dropped: the £9,000 that she had given me for Jonathan's funeral had been taken from her current account. Since then she now had a *'cash flow problem'* so if I had now been granted probate *'it would be most helpful'* if I could *'reimburse'* her.

She rounded the email by sending all her love to me and the boys.

I was stunned.

I read and re-read the email to be absolutely sure that I had read what I thought I had read – but there was no mistake.

Could it really be the case that a mere *six days* after I had buried Jonathan, *her own son,* that Patricia was asking for her money back for the organisation of the funeral? I had just been widowed, left with a three year old and a seven year old – her grandchildren. She knew that financially my situation was not clear and I did not yet have access to Jonathan's funds. But here it was – written in black and white – a reimbursement of her money would be '*most helpful.*'

I was disgusted by her email.

Was this revenge for my not allowing her to set foot inside my house? For not showing enough deference to her and her family? For not allowing myself to be pushed around? Or was she just in the throes of grief and this state was causing her to act unreasonably? I collected myself yet again. It seemed that every time I tried to puncture my way out of the haze and fog of grief, I was prevented from doing so by that family. By her. I composed what I hoped was an appropriate and calm response, my rage and anger seething again underneath the surface.

'Hello Patricia, I am afraid that I am not in a position to reimburse you yet. Jonathan died suddenly and I do not have access to his accounts. Probate has not completed yet and is likely to take a bit more time. Until then I have a serious cash flow problem too.

As for the pantomime, I am sure you will understand when I say that I do not feel up to it. Neither are the two boys for obvious reasons. I will send the photo of Jonathan to Vincent as soon as I receive it. Hopefully this will help him with retaining happy memories of Jonathan. Regards. Thelma.'

Her response was brief and immediate. She acknowledged that she will need to make other arrangements to deal with her cash flow issue. She also understood why I was not keen to attend the pantomime – she did not feel up to it either. She then ended by saying that I should keep in touch and that I was welcome to come and stay with her anytime.

It was notable that although I had specifically pointed out to her in my email that I had a 'serious cash flow problem' too this was ignored by her entirely. A loving mother-in-law may have honed in on this and tried to offer some help especially if they were in a position to offer it. But not Patricia. Even if I had explicitly asked her for help, based on the recent interactions with her, I had a strong hunch what the answer would be.

On reflection I should not have been surprised. I remembered the look on June's face when I had said that I would need funds in order to pay for the funeral at that time – a look that suggested to me her disgust and annoyance – reflecting the attitude of: *'how dare you ask us for money?!'*. This was a family that took a unique position when it came to money. It brought to mind a story that Jonathan had told me once.

We were on one of our many visits to his parents in the Cotswolds when our children were very young, a lifetime ago. We had visited the nearby famous Dales Farm and were having tea in the overpriced restaurant with our two boys. Jonathan had had a small wistful smile on his face as he spoke and relayed his tale. Jonathan had needed money to complete some element of his medical course many years ago when he had been training to be a doctor. There had been 'talk' that Tom would lend him this money. But in the end, Tom did not do so. I did not know what to make of it at the time. But concerning the story Jonathan told me then, I'm ashamed to say that I did not believe him at first – not really. Instead, I thought that there must have been a good reason why his brother would not help him. Or that perhaps Jonathan had antagonised him in some way thereby ensuring that any offer of help was curtailed. Knowing the family the way that I was beginning to know them now, I now believed it.

As I read Patricia's emails again I pondered Jonathan's tale and his family's relationship with money. It certainly created some insight – especially about Jonathan's own position on the subject of money. I had always found him to be a bit on the frugal side – constantly looking for bargains or 'value for money' as he liked to say, in anything that we purchased or bought – whether it be holidays or car insurance. I had found it frustrating at times but had not attributed this behaviour much to his family upbringing. Until now. But although it deepened my understanding of their behaviour it did not completely eliminate the hurt and anger I felt towards them – especially towards Patricia at this point. For me, she had crossed a line in demanding back money used for her own son's funeral less than a week after he had died. I put her email to one side: I would not be visiting anytime soon.

I could feel myself falling. Even as I forged on with all the admin that I still needed to complete post death, I knew that I was reaching the limit of what I could do without some rest and recuperation. So I planned some time away by myself in a nearby hotel to decompress without the children present. I had not had any time away to just to be by myself since Jonathan had died – I really needed to be alone.

With the help of Kathy and Valerie I managed to get away for the night, with Kathy picking up the boys for me from school and then Valerie looking after them at the house whilst I was gone. Finally I would have some respite. I would have time to myself to just think, and breathe, and sleep and cry and just be – without watching myself or putting on a mask for the boys – constantly keeping the veneer of calm for them even whilst inside me there were frequent violent eruptions of emotion.

That day was a busy day. I had errands to run, including a trip to my solicitor's office. I had to hand in various documents relating to Jonathan's bank details and other similar documents. The latter I had found after a diligent search amongst where I thought Jonathan kept all his important paperwork. It was odd going through Jonathan's things and sifting through the detritus of his life before me. Even odder having to hand them to a stranger for the purpose of legal processes to complete probate. In the taxi going back home from the lawyers I felt lightheaded and unfocused. I cried and then stopped abruptly becoming numb again. This was a constant thing which would happen to me almost every day: periods of intense anguish and then almost immediately, as soon as it was expelled – absolutely nothing – just numbness and then detachment. I desperately needed my time away.

Eventually, by early evening, I had arrived at the hotel. I completed check in, found my room and then blissfully closed the door on the world. It was a relief to just be on my own in the hotel room. To not have to pretend in any way. To not have to appear strong, calm and resilient. To just look and feel miserable.

And tired.

And lonely.

It had now been about two weeks since the funeral and six weeks since Jonathan had died. Those 42 days since his death was a lifetime. I felt like I had travelled to another world, a completely different dimension. One that was grey and soulless. Full of loss. Full of sadness.

I did not want to be in this world.

I had chosen a trendy spa hotel near to Westfield. The last time I had visited Westfield was to buy my interview outfit.

And my funeral dress. At the same time. *Stop it. Just try and relax.*

I sat on the king-size bed and looked around the room. It was nice enough with an en suite bath and an office style table and chair. It was surprisingly roomy for a double – had the hotel upgraded me? Most likely but I cared very little at that point. I ordered room service and tried to relax when it arrived. I nursed my glass of wine as I picked at my dinner which was edible but not as satisfying as the merlot I was sampling. I abandoned my plate and continued to sip my wine. It was at that moment, just as I was beginning to feel that I could breathe and unwind that I was hit by another bombshell. I probably should not have brought out my phone to check my emails. But I did. I could not unsee what I saw next.

The short email from Tom carried with it a Word document – an attached letter. The ball of dread that had been present at the funeral swiftly returned. I agonised for a moment. Did I really want to do this now?

I clicked on it.

The letter began by acknowledging the trauma we had all suffered following Jonathan's death before getting down to business. Tom and June made clear from the outset that they were trying to 'balance' their concern for my grief with their own desire to show how my 'behaviour' had caused them pain in order to 'clear the air'. They then set out what they needed to say. They were considerate people who had tried to make me feel welcome as part of their family despite my 'coolness' towards them. I had resisted their offers of help after Jonathan's illness and been 'insensitive' to their pain. Having laid the foundations, the remaining two paragraphs of their letter then set out their attack lines. Despite having a plethora of people to help me including (apparently) nannies, my mother, my sister and them – I had been insistent on sending Jonathan into hospital or to stay with Patricia and in doing so 'fighting Jonathan's wishes'. I did not care for Jonathan sufficiently in hospital, leaving the majority of his care to him and June. And it would seem I had committed the crime of allowing Jonathan's decomposing body to be viewed in church.

They ended by expressing 'regret' about writing to me in this way but hoped that an 'exchange of views' now would better facilitate our relationship in the future. The letter was signed off with 'Best wishes'.

I must have stared into space for only a few minutes – but it felt like an eternity.

Almost immediately I felt physically ill – as though I had been punched in the stomach. I re-read the letter again, and then again, disbelief and anguish coursing through me. The middle part of the letter attacking me acting like lethal targets hitting its mark each time – '*you initially chose to visit him only for short periods* ... '*you allowed Jonathan's decomposing body to be viewed in church.*' I was in tears. How could they do this? How could they send this to me now? At this time? I called my mother. She picked up on the fourth ring. 'Mama.' I said nothing more, I was crying too hard.

'What is it? What's happened?' My mother's voice was sharp, no doubt trying to contain her panic.

'Tom and June ... they sent me a letter ...'

My mother was silent for two beats. 'What did they say now?!' I tried to answer but I was barely coherent as I babbled about what I had just read, only managing to pull myself together long enough to send her a copy via email whilst still on the phone with her. She rang off to read the letter and then called me back a few minutes later. By now my sobbing had stopped but I was still leaking tears. I listened to my mother as she raged at Tom and June and that 'whole damned family' whilst at the same time trying to console me. By the time she hung up I was exhausted. My equilibrium was completely shattered. So much for having some rest and respite. As weary and as tired as I was, as broken as I was, for this family I would have to don my armour and go into battle again. Through rage and tears and weariness, I drafted my response immediately. I decided to let rip and tell them everything that was on my mind.

> *'Tom and June, I have read your letter with disbelief and I am deeply upset and saddened. You start by saying that you are considerate and inclusive people. You are both clearly not. But I will come back to that in a moment.*
>
> *Let me begin by addressing what you say in your letter to me.*
>
> 1. *You say when 'Jonathan became ill you resisted our offers of help.' That is not true. I don't recall any offer of help from you. I do recall asking you for help one evening when I had been left to fend for Jonathan and the 2 boys on my own and you were completely unhelpful, patronising and oblivious to my plight.*
> 2. *You say that I had the help of nannies, my sister and my mother during the time that Jonathan was ill. This is not true. I was ON MY OWN. My mother and sister were not there. The nannies were no longer employed by us. I was desperate and on my own and you, his brother, made no effort to come until the end.*
> 3. *You say that I was intent on ignoring Jonathan's wishes and sending him to hospital. I was distraught. Jonathan*

was deteriorating before my very eyes and as I pointed out above – I was on my own with two young children. You certainly weren't there and are in no position to judge me. I wanted him to get well and honestly thought he should be in hospital. I don't have your experience of hospitals – all I knew was that he needed help. Your insinuation is insulting and deeply upsetting.

4. *When Jonathan went into hospital I was about to contact you that very same morning but you had already found out that he was in hospital. So that is a lie.*

5. *You say that I chose to visit him for short periods when I found out he was dying. It was half term, I had the boys to look after as you very well know and I had to constantly manage the arrangements in order to spend as much time as I could with Jonathan. How dare you suggest that I was not doing enough. What you imply is so heartbreaking.*

6. *On the day of the funeral I did exclude you from the house. It was necessary for Dominic's mental health and welfare. I would do the same again without hesitation as my boys' mental health comes first.*

7. *I did allow Jonathan's body to be viewed. You saw the amount of people who chose to view Jonathan. They were shocked by his death and the speed of it and they needed the viewing for closure. Many of his colleagues thanked me for allowing that and Charles, the priest, specifically told me afterwards that he thought it was the right thing to have a viewing because of the outpouring of grief from everyone. So whilst I understand your point I will stand by the decision I made and that decision was the correct one.*

In some ways I am glad that you have written this letter because it gives me an opportunity to point out a few things about you and your family's behaviour which has been noted by many, many people including his colleagues and by Dominic (unprompted by me I might add although I am in full agreement):

1. *You left me on my own to look after Jonathan in his last dying weeks whilst you stayed in your home in Oxfordshire. You only came down for one weekend and then you finally came to the hospital where admittedly you and June were good in looking after Jonathan when I could not because of the two boys. Despite the latter however, your initial reticence in doing more for your brother was striking and quite frankly appalling. Many kept asking me why you were not there sooner and I had no response to this because, let's face it, there is no good response.*

2. *During the funeral you chose not to help carry the coffin back to the hearse. I was shocked and disgusted by this. He was your brother and yet you and your sons could not afford him that final courtesy.*

3. *During the funeral it was noted by many, including Dominic, the way you all left abruptly and particularly for Dominic, who is old enough to acknowledge this, noted that his own cousins, your children, made NO ATTEMPT to speak to their recently bereaved cousins. This is just so hurtful and again unforgivable.*

4. *You come across as affable and caring when you are with the boys but yet you have shown absolutely no interest in your nephews since their father's death. Jonathan died on 25 October. It is now 7 December. Not once in all that*

time have you demonstrated the emotional intelligence
of a caring uncle. Let me provide some evidence:
   (1) *How many times have you asked to speak to the boys*
      since Jonathan's death, especially Dominic? None
   (2) *How many times have you written a card or little*
      letter to the boys since Jonathan's death? None
   (3) *How many times have you asked to come to visit*
      to see how we are all doing as we are in intense
      grief, especially the boys who are breaking my
      heart with their tears and sorrow? None

I could go on and on (and believe me I am really tempted to
do so) but I am going to stop here Tom and I will do so for
one simple reason: Jonathan. I am mourning him and the
pain of his departure tears new wounds in me every day.
The way that you, June, Patricia and your 3 children have
behaved towards me and my two boys has been nothing
short of disgraceful. Your letter demonstrates this.

So I will stop this now. From today, after your letter, I
am going to take my time to mourn without any further
upset or interruption from you or Patricia. You will not
hear from me during this period for however many weeks,
months, or more that it will take. I will not allow you or
Patricia to upset me and the boys any more during this
very difficult period. Enough is enough. Shame on you
all. Thelma.'

I was in fight or flight mode – I could not help myself. It is
strange that even after all this time I sometimes still view
the letter as a hostile missive rather than a peace offering.
Then again, on other occasions, depending on my mood,
when I read the letter I can see that words have been written

precisely for the benefit of conveying a more conciliatory tone. The letter after all says that the intention was one of attempted reconciliation. When I reflect now I do ask myself – was I too harsh in my response? Should I have taken the time to consider its contents very carefully before replying rather than automatically seeing it as an attack? In other words, should I have trusted the intention of the letter instead of viewing it as a malice-ridden poison pen letter designed to cause maximum hurt and pain to me? Well there is no doubt that if I had taken their letter at face value the course of our relationship may be very different to the way it is now. However, this was not the case. I was a new widow. I was raw. I had just buried my husband a mere 14 days ago. To then be subject to a forensic assessment of my behaviour during the period of Jonathan's illness and funeral was always likely to make me absolutely furious.

It also almost broke me.

I was in bits for days afterwards. My mother, in a rare moment of intervention, also felt compelled to write to Tom and June after their email to me – giving me the much needed support that I craved at that point. Her own email, sent to them via me, was more to the point stating that my grief and sadness was still raw and that I did not need them 'rubbing salt' into it. She reminds Tom that he had not wanted to get involved with the funeral arrangements, deciding instead to defer any offer of help to June so he had no right now to criticise my efforts in organising the funeral. She ends the email with fury: '*As the children's uncle, you did not once call or make contact to find out how they were doing; how they were managing. Not once! I do not want my daughter to be someone you can upset when you feel like. Please leave my daughter alone!*'

In terms of communication from the in-laws, I thought that the email from Tom and June would be it – but this was not the case. In what appears to be a coordinated pincer movement, I received an email from Patricia herself. This arrived the next day, after I had returned home from my unsuccessful retreat at the spa hotel. A softer version of her son's brutal letter but nonetheless adopting the same theme of telling me how I had wronged them and pointing out, ever so gently, the errors of my ways.

The email from Patricia began with concern and empathy for me and the boys as well as an exploration of her and Vincent's grief and suffering. She demonstrates real sensitivity towards me and the boys in the first part of her letter, saying, '*Our feelings of grief do not diminish our compassion for your loss and for the grief that you and the children are suffering. We acknowledge the anxiety and bewilderment you must be feeling at the prospect of bringing up two sons without the help and guidance of their father.*' But then – the tone of the letter changed.

Although she thanks me for the photograph of Jonathan that I had sent to Vincent, she does so whilst noting that it had been sent to only him, evidence that my relationship with her was strained. She goes on to say, '*without rancour and blame*' that my behaviour at times had caused her and Vincent '*unnecessary pain and unhappiness.*' She adds that I was likely to say the same of her behaviour too and that a lot of the reason for this was that we had approached the situation from different perspectives – that her 'balance of concern' had been towards Jonathan's welfare whereas mine had been towards that of the boys – thereby making each of us '*less sensitive to each other's anxiety and grief.*' Even though the hurt and pain would diminish in time, for now though we must be '*honest with each other and not allow ill feeling to affect our relationship.*'

She goes on to say that she hoped we would all come together as a family and put away our grievances towards each other, recognising that the 'grief and pain' over Jonathan's illness had led to our subsequent actions. Their love and devotion to me and the boys was still present and that our priority now was to provide the supportive environment that the boys needed. To demonstrate this she ends by inviting me and the boys to visit her and Vincent during the New Year (adding that Tom and June would like that too), so that we can all '*start the New Year as we wish to go on, bringing the family together in mutual love, respect and support.*'

In fairness, her email did not pull its punches but seemed to be written with love and care. On its own, I probably would have been prepared to give it a fair hearing. There was just one problem – it appeared to me to be sent as a combined effort with her son and therefore I saw it as part of the same campaign. I did not respond to it and dismissed it as nothing more than her version of good cop to Tom's bad cop: I was not going to fall for it. In the interim, Tom and June had been busy crafting and sending their response to my email and my mother's email. Their email was brief, a mere few lines stating that my mother and I had misinterpreted their letter: they had actually been offering an '*olive branch*'. They continue, much like Patricia had said in her email, that in order to move forward we needed to be honest with each other concerning the problems '*festering under the surface*' and '*to do this in a non-aggressive and non-pejorative way.*' They round it off by saying they were ready to talk. Best wishes again.

I considered Tom and June's new email for a day or so. I wonder how much I tried to believe them. I am not sure, truth be told, I ever seriously entertained the possibility that they could be genuine. That perhaps they did have good intentions but their clumsy wording had created the opposite effect of what they intended. All I knew, all I felt at that time was that, rightly or wrongly, I was under attack. I thought *'who the hell are they to lecture me and point out my mistakes whilst I am going through hell?!'* I suppose playing devil's advocate, one could say that even if they felt they had valid points to make – and I admit that I had not always acted in a benign manner towards them throughout this whole affair – one would have to question the timing of their letter. Was it really necessary for them to send this letter so soon after I had buried Jonathan when I would be at my most vulnerable? In the end, I think that the letter would always receive a frosty reception from me, but maybe I would have had a bit more of an open mind had they timed the sending of the letter better – perhaps a few months after Jonathan died when the dust had settled.

Not 14 days after I had buried my husband.

In the end, that letter set off a chain reaction in me. My upset and rage began to crystallise. I was vulnerable yes – but that did not mean that I would have to be a sitting duck for my in-laws whenever they felt the need to attack me or prod me or poke me. Over the day or two that followed since the latest emails and letters from my in-laws I became more and more incensed. And the more incensed I became the more depressed it made me that I could be affected in this way. *For pity's sake – don't I have enough to be dealing with right now?!*

It was during my second day of stewing over the contents of their correspondence that I suddenly had a eureka moment. I was on my way to the Royal Free Hospital. I had decided to utilise the services of the cancer charity Maggie's, which offered support to people with cancer and their loved ones. Not because I felt that I was particularly ready to use them – I don't think I was – it just happened to be on my current to-do list and I was at that time blindly following whatever was on that list. Or 'keeping busy' as my sister-in-law had advised me to do the day after my husband had died. Well, that was the only advice of hers that I was willing to take. As I came out of Hampstead Heath overground station and marched to the hospital, I suddenly made up my mind – I did not want any more contact with my in-laws. They had exhausted me, hurt me and pushed me close to the edge of my sanity.

Enough was enough.

I called my lawyer as I navigated the crowds outside the hospital. Thankfully she was sympathetic to my request. I decided to draft and send an email to them now – to get it out of the way. I stopped in front of the hospital and sat on a bench. I typed quickly – trying to be matter of fact and succinct in my response. I knew that I was throwing a hand grenade into the mix but at that moment I did not care. I finished the email and sent it, ensuring my lawyer also had a copy. Relief coursed through me.

'Tom/Patricia, You have both caused me and the boys immeasurable pain. The latest missive from Tom a mere two weeks after I buried Jonathan and whilst I was in the early stages of grief, accusing me of not looking after Jonathan properly, not having Jonathan's best interests at heart, neglecting Jonathan, allowing his decomposing body to be viewed in church etc. ... was for me, the final straw. I am a grieving widow with two very young children and yet the contempt that your family has shown me has been absolutely devastating. Just because you top and tail a letter with 'lots of love' does not make the terrible accusations you make within it any less disturbing or distressing.

I said in my response to Tom that I will now take the time to mourn properly with the children. But I have realised that whilst I don't intend to communicate with you during this period this will not stop either of you from continuing to contact me or continuing your campaign of recriminations against me.

Therefore, having considered the situation very carefully I have decided to take legal advice from my lawyers. We have agreed that to ensure that my boys and I are kept safe from any further upset from both of you during our period of mourning, you will cease all communications directly with me. From now on, if you feel you must communicate with me on any issue during this period of mourning then you will do so via my lawyer.

...

Rebecca [my lawyer] has also been copied into this email.

Please give my regards to Vincent. From both of you however I expect you now to show some respect and keep your distance whilst the boys and I start trying to process what has happened. If you fail to do so, I will seek further legal advice on how to proceed. Thelma.'

I felt I had for the first time taken back control of the situation and maybe given myself some breathing space from them. I walked into Maggie's with a lighter spring in my step.

The eventual response from Patricia came a few days later sent to me via my lawyer. Patricia expressed *'deep regret'* that I had decided to seek legal advice and rejected their attempts to reconcile without *'rancour or blame'* (that expression again!) the disagreements that had arisen between us following the illness and death of Jonathan. She added that Tom and June also felt the same way. Patricia went on to say that she would respect my request to be able to mourn in peace but she hoped that we could still come together as a family for Dominic and Richard. She expressed her wish to be able to continue sending presents and gifts to the boys at Christmas and other special occasions ending with the respectable *'Please will you let us know if Thelma will find this acceptable.'*

Her email was signed off with her full title OBE – no doubt so the lawyers knew whom they were dealing with.

Well.

Still defiant in the end but with an acceptance that I wanted and needed my space to mourn and to just be. I was grateful for that at least. But my good mood was short lived.

Now that I had a little bit of breathing space I was faced with one of the big realities of death – having to cope with the many 'firsts'. The first birthdays without Jonathan. The first anniversary of his death. And of course, the one that was fast approaching now – the first Christmas without Jonathan. Or more specifically my first Christmas as a widow.

CHAPTER 9

The Escape

Normally at Christmastime we, as in Jonathan and I with Dominic and Richard, would troop down to my mother whereupon she would regale us with her fine cooking of turkey with all the trimmings: brussels sprouts with chestnuts, roast potatoes, Christmas pudding and all the other assortment of dishes necessary to create the perfect Christmas meal. After Christmas Day and Boxing Day we normally then went to Patricia and Vincent's house and stayed with them for a few days, during which Tom and his family would visit. On paper it certainly sounded like an ideal way to spend Christmas. Certainly from Dominic and Richard's point of view it probably was. For my part, I always viewed it rather differently. Christmastime was not a period that I necessarily looked forward to but it was also not a time that I always dreaded and wanted to avoid. This year however would be very different.

The whole lead up to Christmas felt very surreal. Autumn had receded and winter had taken its place. Jonathan had been gone almost two months. The boys had resumed their routine of going to school and nursery. I continued my routine of looking after them and taking them to their extracurricular clubs and afterschool events. In one way it was almost as though nothing had changed, especially during the weekdays which were often a flurry of activity. It was the weekends that was the worst. We could not escape the extra silence at that time highlighting in technicolour that something was not right – that there was something or someone missing. And of course, even worse, we gradually became more and more bombarded by Christmas – Christmas carols, Christmas adverts, Christmas parties. Until now I had never really appreciated the extent to which Christmas is entangled with family and family life. Actually, not so much entangled but completely and utterly synonymous with it. The message was loud and clear: Christmas IS family. We could not escape it.

I felt suffocated.

My mother came to stay with me and the boys several days before Christmas Day, and I must admit to being very happy to have her there. I felt a little less lonely having someone else in the house. It was also good to just have another adult to help me with the boys. And to add some noise to the eerie quiet that had descended on our house after Jonathan's death.

On Christmas Eve, I took the boys to the Christingle children's service at my church. When I went there with the boys, I did not really know what to expect. As always during that period I wanted and needed a distraction for myself and for my boys. I was met with kindness by one parent couple, whose daughter was in the same class as Dominic. The husband came to where we were sitting. A tall man with dark hair, balding at the sides and with glasses perched high up on his nose. He moved with the harassed air of a father trying to maintain a conversation whilst trying to keep track of his two young children.

'Would you like to spend Christmas with our family? You would be very welcome.' His eyes were filled with concern.

I did not know him very well. Jonathan's death had definitely resulted in people reaching out to me in ways I could not have fathomed before. I was touched by his kindness.

'That's so nice of you but we are spending Christmas Day with my mother.'

'Well you are very welcome if you change your mind. You know the boys will be alright.' He paused as he shifted his weight from carrying his youngest child. 'I lost my father when I was very young. I remember it being very hard on my mother. We managed to get through it. They will too.'

It is extraordinary how much you learn about people when you have experienced trauma. The way that it opens people up to sharing their own experiences. Here in just a few short weeks I had learnt of another person, after Penny, the friendly nanny who had hugged me so kindly on the night my husband had died, who had also lost their parent at a young age. It made me so sad to realise that my boys would now be joining that club – a club where, having made an appearance in their lives from such a young age, grief and death would now stay with them throughout their lives, forever stalking them as they grow into adulthood.

'Thelma, would you be able to do a reading?' I was broken out of my reverie by Sophie, the other priest at the church. I had only had contact with Charles over the past few months. I hadn't seen Sophie much at all. She looked at me expectantly. I was a little bit confused by her request. I wondered if she knew that I was recently widowed and probably not the best person to do a reading. On the other hand perhaps she was asking me because she knew, and she wanted to engage me in the service. Whatever the reason, I realised that it made little difference. There was no reason why I shouldn't. As I stood at the front reading the holy scripture from the Bible, my hands shook as I held the lesson. I felt completely out of my comfort zone.

And yet.

I embraced it because it was another distraction, another reason to just forget who I was for just a small fraction of time before I faced Christmas Day itself.

I do not remember much about that first Christmas Day. I do remember that having Christmas at my house did not feel right. After my sister arrived to spend the day with us, largely for the boys' benefit, I passed the time trying to feel joyous and happy when I felt anything but. The main thing for me was that I had company – not being left alone with the boys as I usually was.

A few days after Christmas, my mother had to leave. She had been with me for some time now and I really did not want her to go.

'Can't you stay a bit longer?'

'Ngozi, I am old,' she said firmly. 'I need to go back to my own bed. You will be OK.'

Then, having already packed her things, she left, promising to call me soon.

I suppose it may not have been reasonable to expect her to stay indefinitely but I felt utterly alone and dejected by her departure. I could have done with more familial support – from her and from my sister. But instead, my mother went back to her home and what followed was one of the most miserable Christmas periods I have ever experienced. That spell between the end of Boxing Day and the New Year comprised of many, *many* days where there really was not much to do – it was completely empty. Once upon a time, that stretch of time would have been filled with visits to Jonathan's family. As much as I found those visits difficult at times at least we were doing what the vast majority of the population were doing at that exact same time.

Spending time with loved ones.

Spending time with family.

It would not be the case this year.

I tried again to soldier on during that period, taking the boys out for the day to the V&A museum and the Natural History Museum after Boxing Day but before the New Year was upon us. I felt a deep emptiness inside me as I took them round, tried to get them enthused in the children's activities taking place and then sat them down to lunch. Many times I would feel tears pricking my eyes, sometimes escaping and rolling down my face and I would make discreet efforts to wipe them away without the boys noticing. I was deeply unhappy but in some sort of sadistic way I felt I had to go out with the boys and try to have 'fun' and carry on as though Jonathan was still here.

I was relieved in many ways when the New Year came. Not because I was looking forward to it at all. No – it was just a relief to get out of the awful Christmastime, 'season of good will' hell. At least in the New Year I would have something to focus on – my new job.

           ❧ ❧ ❧

It was such a bitter sweet thing that I had landed a job – that I had managed to kickstart my legal career in the City again. The job offer had come shortly after the second interview with the same law firm who had shown interest in me a mere few weeks after Jonathan had died. As with the first interview, I had prepared fastidiously for the second, focusing any spare time and energy on the interview process. When I had left the RAF a year ago and had felt listless – the prospect of starting a job had seemed so alien and scary. Now, remarkably, despite everything (maybe *because* of everything) I was fired up and really wanted to go back to work. That was one thing that Jonathan had supported me in throughout the time we were together – progression in my legal career. However, this was not how I had envisioned things – my working and looking after two young children on my own: Jonathan was supposed to be in this scenario.

But he was gone.

I was in an incredibly febrile state. On the one hand I felt weighed down by grief and felt a gnawing emptiness inside me. On the other hand, I acted as though everything was normal and busied myself with the practicalities of a return to work – an important part of which of course was to hire a nanny to help out. I was a widow now, which meant I was on my own. I could no longer rely on someone who could pick up the reigns if I was at a meeting or had to go to work early or had to stay at work late. I needed someone to do the pick-ups and drop-offs and all the extracurricular activities in between. Unfortunately Valerie could help me occasionally but could not be available all the time. I needed to hire someone new. In the end the search for a nanny was brief. The agency I eventually used managed to help me find someone who could do those odd hours. Another Romanian nanny like Valerie – somehow that filled me with comfort. It was an element of continuity at least.

That left me free to actually start work and oh my, what a start that was. A few weeks after Christmas, once the New Year glow had worn off, I found myself in a room with several other new recruits undergoing my induction into the new firm. It felt amazing. And nerve-racking. At the end of the first day, after undergoing computer training and after spending hours becoming familiar with the laptops which we were all due to take home, I felt very tired. I wondered belatedly how

I was going to manage the whole process of having to work in an office again, having no time to myself in the day, having to travel and commute to work every day. I felt so overwhelmed in that moment.

And yet.

As I left for home after my first full day of work, as I crossed the busy road and headed to the tube station, I also felt wonderful, almost euphoric. I soon realised the reason why: this workplace, this brand new shiny environment was my escape hatch from my life.

No one at work knew about my situation.

No one knew that Jonathan had died from cancer a mere three weeks after diagnosis. No one knew that I was struggling to process what had happened. No one knew that I was trying to manage the grief of my two young sons. No one knew that I was completely alone in doing all this. Here, in this new world I was just another legal recruit, a newly hired Assistant Solicitor on probation. I was normal here. Not a widow. Not an object of pity. It was as though I had taken on the persona of someone else.

And it felt good.

My new job was an environment where I could throw myself into it and not think about or deal with what had happened in my life a mere few months ago. I protected my status by telling absolutely *no one* that my husband had recently died. As I became knee deep in work, becoming accustomed to new work calendars, team meetings, chargeable targets, more induction, lots of legal training, client files, recordable hours and so on I continued the subterfuge. It was liberating to be focused on something else other than my life, to surround myself in a huge open plan office where I was working with a hundred others as opposed to being at home by myself with my thoughts for company. I wanted to escape and be someone else – and at work I was precisely that and for the large part I really enjoyed it. I was back in the City again, and I could pretend, if only for a little while, that nothing bad had happened to me.

Unfortunately, I could not escape entirely. It was a few weeks into my job, whilst I was having lunch in the cafeteria overlooking the River Thames that my phone rang.

'Hi Thelma, how are you?' The familiar male voice jolted me back into the present. It was David, Jonathan's former colleague. David had a special way of talking: he always did so with a lot of care, as though he did not want to offend or step on anyone's toes. At the same time he possessed a steely determination when he wanted something. Eventually, he got to the crux of what he wanted.

'I don't know if you remember but I said that we at the hospital wanted to hold a memorial service for Jonathan. It's really for the patients and staff at the hospital who knew him and weren't able to make the funeral. We wondered if you would be able to come?'

'Oh, right. OK.' I did remember him mentioning something about organising a service for Jonathan sometime in February, around the time of Jonathan's birthday.

'It would be really lovely if you could come. Of course you wouldn't have to do anything – we would do everything and sort out the order of service. It would just be nice if you could come and maybe say a few words?.'

I didn't know how I felt about that at first. Then I warmed to the idea. This would be my chance to say some things about Jonathan and I, something that had been denied of me by Tom and his hurtful eulogy.

'Yes alright David, I can do that.'

I took a thrill out of knowing that I would be able to speak and have my say – finally. As for Jonathan's family, David did not mention them at all to me – neither their knowledge of this memorial service nor their attendance. I was glad of it. I hoped that they were not attending. I could not face them. But even if they were, they could not stop me from speaking – and I had a lot to say.

The memorial service was still several weeks away but I wanted to be prepared. I started considering what I was going to cover in my speech and began the process of drafting it. At this point I had been enjoying the radio silence from the family. I should have known that this simply would not last. The email that came from Patricia via my lawyer, a week after my conversation with David, started innocently enough, beginning as it did with her sending her love to me and the boys, expressing her hope that we could all eventually reconcile in the future, and noting that the differences which had arisen between us was almost inevitable given the suddenness of Jonathan's illness and death. So far, so caring.

But there was more.

She and Vincent had compiled a photo album chronicling Jonathan's life from birth. She thought it would be good for Dominic and Richard as an anniversary present for Jonathan's birthday which was fast approaching on 14 February. She had enclosed a copy of the album in digital format for me to look at in advance – to ensure that I and the boys were ready for the gift.

I paused before opening the file. I was on my bed, just about to unwind for the night. I had been trying to change my sleep routine by getting into the habit of going to bed early. Especially now that I no longer had the option of catching up on rest later on in the day when the children were at school and nursery. Did I really want to open this now? What if it was another can of worms? *This can definitely wait – it's almost 11 pm – go to bed now, you need to rest!*

I clicked on the attachment.

As I scrolled through the photo album attached I became more and more upset. It was not just the inaccuracies which bothered me (Jonathan had gone into hospital *after* she and Tom had visited – not *during* their visit as the narrative in the album had indicated), it was also the way that I had been completely airbrushed out of the picture when it came to Jonathan's last few hours. It was Patricia, Vincent, Tom and June who had been by his bedside it would seem – not me at all. Hurt and anger competed with each other inside me. *When was this going to end? When?!* If she had taken a hammer and swung it at me I doubt that she could have caused more damage than this awful album. As I drafted my response, tears pricked my eyes but my heart and my head were cold with rage:

> *'Patricia, When Tom and June sent me that devastating letter they did not put you down as a signatory. However, I am sure that you were instrumental in drafting that letter. Well, in the light of the photo album you have sent, I feel that it is my turn to say a few things.*
>
> 1. *There is an overriding lack of respect for me and the role that I have played in Jonathan's life and death by you and your family. Your photo album demonstrates this. It is also deeply distressing.*
>   (a) *Firstly, it is inaccurate. Jonathan became ill during the Monday night and not the Sunday that you visited him. I called the ambulance in the early*

hours of the morning of Tuesday 22 October (twice
– Jonathan refused to go the first time I called the
ambulance even though he was throwing up water
and was in terrible pain). I made sure he got to
hospital when he needed it because I could see that
he was in such pain that could not be managed at
home. I did this. Not Tom. Not June.

(b) *It also leaves out important details:*

- *It leaves out the fact that I cared for Jonathan for*
  2 and a half weeks every night and every day by
  myself with two young children in tow.
- *It leaves out the fact that I was at the hospital*
  every single day along with Tom and June.
- *Before he wrote that appalling letter, Tom*
  indicated that he knew the role that I had played
  in caring for Jonathan. On the 25 October, after
  Jonathan had died, when he drove me back to
  my house, I thanked him for all the effort he and
  June had put into looking after Jonathan. He
  responded by saying that I had done all the hard
  work in looking after Jonathan at home by myself
  previously. He conveniently forgot this when he
  wrote that letter to me.

(c) *You include the beautiful reading that I chose for*
the funeral service in your photo album but again
you omit to mention that it was I who chose that
reading because it was I who organised the beautiful
ceremony for Jonathan all by myself. Not you. Not
Tom. Not June.

2. *The ongoing theme of airbrushing me out of Jonathan's life*
and ignoring the crucial role that I have played within it

was already there at the funeral. During the eulogy that you and Tom wrote, I was barely mentioned even though I am his wife and I looked after Jonathan, and was his primary carer during the whole period he was unwell until he went into hospital.

In particular you have forgotten that it was I who:

- Took him to his hospital appointments
- Went shopping for him every day to buy him supplies
- Cared for him at night
- Cared for him during the day
- Gave him his pain medications and so on.

And did all that whilst trying to look after two young children. On my own. Without you. Without Tom. Without June. Not mentioning this in an album that you have created and want to give to my own sons is hurtful, disrespectful and rude.

Well, I have decided that [Dominic] should not receive a hard copy of the photo album, at least not in its present form. Leaving aside all of the above, even if your narrative was completely fair and accurate, surely you must realise that [Dominic] is absolutely not ready for this? He is just a 7 year old boy who is grieving and going through child bereavement counselling. This is too much for him.

I will show [Dominic] the photos when he is ready (when he is much older and after speaking to the childhood bereavement counsellor to ensure he is ready). And even then I will only show him the photos with the small captions or the narratives talking about other aspects of Jonathan's life. Not the narratives talking about his death. This would overwhelming for an adult let alone a child.

In the meantime, I want to continue to take time to grieve with my two sons. This process would be made much easier if you resisted the temptation to contact me through my lawyer unless it was absolutely necessary. Thelma.'

When I received no immediate response from her I was relieved. Perhaps now this would be the end of it. Save for the February memorial (which I began to dread as the time came nearer) when I would have to deal with them if they attended, I honestly believed that I would hear no more. I was glad. I hated Patricia at that moment. I hated her and her whole family and the way that they seemed to seize every opportunity to upset me in some way. It is said that anger is one of the stages of grief. I had no doubt that I was right in the midst of that stage – embracing it with each new fight and in doing so, unable to really move forward.

The simmering anger towards the family and my new job worked together to distract me, to keep me focused on things other than my enveloping sadness and depression. Work was all-consuming and new – it was a tonic. As I navigated office life again, the perils and pitfalls of working and in particular, open plan offices, I began to come into my own. I felt proud of myself for managing to go back to lawyering again. I felt proud of myself that I was able to call myself a lawyer again. And with each occasion that I commuted to and from work, I felt proud of what I had achieved given that a mere few months ago I had been unemployed and looking for work. Now, here I was, striding into my job with purpose. Focused on case analysis, legal research, organising case files, getting to grips with the online document management system that all staff had to use and much more.

And still no one knew.

And whilst they remained ignorant I carried on with forging a new identity for myself as a lawyer again. And it felt good.

All too soon, February arrived and with it the apprehension returned. February was usually a significant month, being the month of Jonathan's birthday, my own birthday and now, this year, it would be the month of the memorial service organised by David and his colleagues. I had prepared what I thought was appropriate wording for the service. I had laid out in advance the outfit that I would wear. But I was still very, *very* nervous. I had decided given the raw state of the boys it would be best if they did not attend this memorial service – the main funeral was more than enough for them. This was not the case for me. I would, in effect, be reliving another funeral service for my late husband. But more importantly than that, I could, in a short space of time, be exposing myself to crossing the path yet again of Jonathan's family – something I did not want to do. I began to regret how readily I had agreed to this.

There was one positive thing about all this – I would have Amaka at my side as a friend and shoulder to lean on. Amaka was one of the hospital pharmacists who worked closely with Jonathan. Up until that point she had effectively been in the background, being one of those who had visited Jonathan in his dying days at the hospital and then she had done a reading at the funeral. We had only really connected after Jonathan's funeral, when I had received a call from her a few days after the service just as I was doing some light shopping in Kensal Rise straight after the school run:

'I just wanted to say that Jonathan was so loved and respected by all those who knew him. The patients didn't always understand him, thinking he was a bit abrupt and rude sometimes. But when they later enquired about outstanding matters they always found that it was Jonathan who had advocated for them. It was Jonathan who had cared deeply for their plight.' She paused, taking stock, her emotions coming to the fore.

I paused as I listened to her, slowing down my pace as I walked towards the shops. Yet again I was hearing the same story about my late husband – how he was well respected, well regarded, how his patients were affected deeply by him – in a positive way. Why did I not know any of this? Jonathan rarely, if ever, spoke about his day, about what had occurred or even about his patients in any great depth. Not for the first time I felt estranged from him and wondered at how little I knew him.

'I would really like to come and visit you and see how you are.'

I was not especially keen. I felt that I had had my fill of visits. 'Honestly, its fine. I am doing OK. It's really not necessary.'

'No please, I would like to, Jonathan was like family to us – it would really mean a lot to me ...'

I could not say no to that. We arranged a convenient time for her to come and I carried on with my errands.

But on the day that she was due to come I was not in a great state to receive visitors. I had been in the process of sorting out all of Jonathan's admin, including going through the laborious process of organising all of Jonathan's affairs and transferring everything of note including household bills into my sole name. I decided that afternoon to pull out all of Jonathan's paperwork and had created piles of paper on the living room carpet grouped according to subject areas: water bills, electricity bills, household insurance etc. When the bell rang I moved reluctantly to the front door, hoping that the visit would not take too long so I could return to the task at hand. She came in, looking tall and beautiful, immaculately laid out, in sharp contrast to me – washed out and tired. She took in the papers on the floor at a glance. I started to move the paperwork out of the way, inwardly cursing the fact that I had started this task now, the very same afternoon that I knew she would be coming. In any event she was warm and kind, and easy to talk to. We talked about Jonathan and she offered support which was nice of her. We bonded over our common Nigerian heritage and talked about a number of things including our children. I expressed my fears with her:

'I have this house and I don't know what I am going to do with it. I don't even know how to access the loft – Jonathan always managed to go up there. I don't know what I am going to do!' It was very random, but it was one of the many things that was constantly on my mind – the common theme being – how on earth was I really going to cope with everything now that Jonathan was gone?

'Don't worry about all that now. It's fine.' Her words were soothing and made me feel better. I liked her.

So as Amaka drove us to the church for the service organised by David, I felt as good as I could be – with her I felt I was in safe hands. She acted as a guide as we picked our way through the path leading to the church entrance. I still felt nervous but I hoped I would be in a safe place with Jonathan's colleagues.

My hope was misplaced.

The hostility towards me when we went inside the church was not overwhelming. But it was not subtle either. It was there in David's forced grin and awkward quick hug. It was there in the slightly averted eyes of Jonathan's colleagues – the smile that did not reach their eyes. I wondered if I was wrong in my perception but no, I felt my instincts were correct – they were not particularly happy to see me. This baffled me more than upset at the time: I barely knew them and couldn't imagine what I might have done to upset them but with Amaka at my side acting as interference and giving me strength I put my feelings to one side. Because I also had another feeling to contend with, one which was much more welcome – relief: Patricia and her family were not here. Their possible presence had been playing on my mind, causing me quite a bit of discomfort and sometimes panic. However, I needn't have worried – they were not here. I was grateful for their absence.

As I sat down I looked through the order of service. This was clearly David's effort, and by his own admission, was cobbled together from the original order of service that I had created for the main funeral. The photos of me and Jonathan and the boys were again there: the beautiful photo that I had taken when we were in France, the selfie showing all of us smiling together, squashed together to ensure we were all in the frame. I put it down and started to cry and then stopped myself. Amaka squeezed my hand comfortingly.

The service started and it soon became a blur. Patients then fellow doctors started talking about Jonathan, saying how wonderful he was as a doctor, how he had changed their lives. I remember one of the patients spoke eloquently about Jonathan, just as he had at the main funeral he had attended. I wish I could remember more of who spoke and about what at that service but I was frozen in a bubble of grief and impending fear. Soon I would be speaking and frankly, despite my training as a lawyer, the prospect of standing up and speaking filled me with terror. I wanted to crawl away and hide. Not for the first time I fervently wished I had not agreed to this. But soon I was up. I went up to the front. I felt no confidence at all. Even as I walked up I sensed again the hostility towards me. I opened the piece of paper I had printed off, and with my hands visibly shaking, I read what I had drafted and redrafted over the course of the past few weeks. Brief words but words which nonetheless I struggled to get out, at one point breaking down in tears:

'*Hello everyone,*

Thank you all for coming to this service to celebrate Jonathan's life and to mark his sudden and unexpected death.

Jonathan was an extraordinary man. And I say that not just because I was his wife. But because that is the truth. He was equally talented in the sciences and in the arts. He was passionate and driven in all that he pursued whether it was his research project, or his guitar playing or his sculpture and artwork or even his running: in everything he did he pursued it with a vigour and enthusiasm that many could not match. He was also humble in many ways because the immense achievements that he made at work and the difference that he made in the lives of so many of his patients, many of whom are here, he barely spoke of and that just reflects the kind of person he was. He was like a rough diamond: maybe a little rough on the outside but an absolute gem on the inside.

A day after his diagnosis, I told him that in addition to all that he had achieved, that his greatest legacy, and he has many legacies I know, but the greatest ones would be his two children, Dominic our 7 year old and Richard our 3 year old, who loved their father so very much, as did I. He will be with us always.

Today is Jonathan's birthday and he would have been 60 had he still been with us. Well, today we will mourn but we will also celebrate his life and his work and remember him how he was. I am sure that is what he would have wanted.

Thank you'

I was relieved when I came to the end and was able to sit back down.

I had managed to do it.

I felt liberated in an odd sort of way in comparison to the first funeral that I had organised but in which I had not spoken. This time, free from the shackles of management and administration, I was able to actually take part, to give voice to my thoughts and my grief. In that I took some solace. Amaka gave me a comforting pat well done. The rest of the memorial service was on the surface fine. I spoke to a few people and thanked many who came. I was introduced to Max, the doctor who would be spearheading the work of Jonathan and bringing his beloved project to fruition. Despite the resentment I felt towards Jonathan about his project, I still felt very much compelled to push for it to be completed. It was almost as though I was Jonathan's champion, my sense of loyalty trumping my anger towards him for the way I felt he had not always put me first in the past. This sense of loyalty ensured that when I was speaking to the head of the hospital trust I shook her hand and asked her point blank if she was going to provide support for the carrying out of his project. She was rather taken aback, murmuring that the matter would now be overseen by Max – but I felt on Jonathan's behalf, a sense of obligation, even duty to tackle the powers that be on this issue. But still, despite this small triumph, I felt a deep uneasiness at being there amongst his colleagues and it was only as we left and Amaka was driving us away that I felt that I could breathe again. Several days later I discovered the reason for the hostility and uneasiness I had experienced and it came quite out of the blue.

As usual, when I am riding the crest of a wave, something would always happen to make me crash back down to earth.

The email was waiting for me on my mobile when I returned back to my desk after a work meeting and a relatively productive day at work so far. Rebecca, my lawyer, began by apologising for the delay in forwarding to me an email she had received from Patricia several days ago as she had been on half-term leave. An email from Patricia was attached, nestled at the bottom of the page.

I closed my eyes briefly then quickly opened them and scrolled down the email before I could change my mind. It was an email of two halves. The first part of Patricia's email was devoted entirely to how 'distressed and saddened' she and Vincent were about my 'angry and abusive' response to their photo album – one which was apparently compiled '*as an act of love and reconciliation*'. It seems that it was my 'self-obsessed fantasy' which led me to view it as anything other than a celebration of Jonathan's life. She continues that I had never responded to her letter of reconciliation and that in doing so I had appeared to reject that offer and all subsequent offers to reconcile. Even so, she adds that their grief had never diminished their compassion for my grief and loss and that of the boys.

As she moved into the second half of her email, the real reason I would guess that she wrote to me at all, the tone of her email swiftly changed – from hurtful anger to righteous indignation. And rage.

She had just been speaking to David who asked her if she would be attending Jonathan's memorial service – one which he had organised 'presumably' with my help. He assumed that we would all be attending together as a family. My failure to inform her of this memorial service she construed as '*an act of premeditated cruelty*'. She ends with fury, saying that she and Vincent would continue sending gifts to Dominic and

Richard but that she was 'finished and done' with making any more contact with me – adding that she and Vincent were 'simply too old' to deal with my apparent 'self-obsession and indifference' towards them. The email ended with one line: *'we leave it to you to contact us if and when you wish for any future contact with your family.'* No best wishes.

I took my phone and went into the ladies' toilets. The facilities here were sleek, modern and spacious with glittering dark tiles and flattering mirrors. Thankfully, the toilet cubicles were empty. I went into one, closed and locked the door and re-read the email. My heart was pounding. I felt like I had been punched squarely in the stomach. The bubble of brief joy I had enjoyed at my desk slowly and purposefully deflated.

I had been invaded again.

Any time I tried to get on with my life, at every turn, the family would find me. I could not escape.

I sent a copy of the email to my mother and then waited in the toilet stall. For what, I do not know. For my heart to stop pounding. Until I felt that I could move again, that I could walk back to my desk, pick up my files and resume work as though nothing had happened. The hostility I felt at the memorial service made perfect sense now. I clearly had not imagined it. They were all angry with me, blaming me for the fact that Jonathan's family members were not there. David had most likely spoken to Tom. I could just imagine how the conversation went – *'Oh dear, did you not know about the service? I thought that Thelma would have told you ...'* I felt furious with David, feeling oddly a sense of betrayal from him even though I barely knew him – he was after all Jonathan's colleague, not my best friend. But my real ire was reserved for Patricia and the appalling way she treated me and insulted me in the email. Always there to poison my mood and my sanity.

Eventually, I made my way back to my desk and sat down. It was near the end of the day. Thankfully, I did not have long to feign interest in my work emails and in the case file I was reading and rereading. When I left for the day I was in a daze, detached and unfocused during the commute home.

Over the course of the next couple of days, I managed to draft a response. I was shaking with anger as I did. I did not hold back: I meant business. I sent the email to Rebecca who sent it on to Patricia promptly.

Patricia,

This has got to stop. I am struggling to find the space to grieve properly and every email from you is like a hand grenade that you fling into the process.

Let me remind you of what I have experienced from you since Jonathan's death:

1. *Two weeks after his death, a mere two weeks, you write to me (via Tom and June) and say the following things to me:*

   'When Jonathan had to go into hospital, you didn't contact us. When the consultants told us that he was dying, you initially chose to visit him only for short periods and left much of his care entirely to us. On the day of the funeral you excluded us from the house and you allowed Jonathan's decomposing body to be viewed in church.'

   These words are not filled with love and kindness (which you say you have offered me since Jonathan's death). They are filled with blame and anger. I want you to read these words again and imagine that you had received this 14 days after your husband had died. In sending me that email via your son and daughter-in-law you caused me so much emotional pain and suffering. I still feel that intense pain now when I see those words written again. You cannot send that kind of email to someone who has just lost their husband, 3 weeks after a diagnosis of cancer and think that it can be swept aside as mere 'differences'. The email was cruel. And it hurts. It still does. It is because of that email that we are in the position that we are in now. Be in no doubt about that.

2. *Prior to that email, you were rude and dismissive when I told you that there should be no one in the house on the day of the funeral because of the distress it would cause [Dominic]. [Dominic] was wonderful during the funeral itself but do you have any idea what it was like that morning getting ready? [Dominic] was an absolute wreck. The tears and the anguish we had to go through to get outside the house I cannot begin to describe to you. And yet in your WhatsApp message you say 'We do not wish to be denied access to the house. The idea is monstrous.' Your own needs were more important than anyone else.*

3. *In the eulogy that I mentioned in my last email to you, I was deliberately barely mentioned. Jonathan and I were married for the best part of a decade! This was so utterly painful having to sit through and listen to it at my own husband's funeral. How would you feel if you were barely mentioned in a eulogy when your husband had recently passed away? Knowing the kind of person you are I cannot imagine for a second that you would find that acceptable. And yet this is what you did to me.*

Subsequent emails professing love and affection cannot heal the wound. How can you not see that?

4. *You make a photo album where in the narrative concerning Jonathan's death you minimise my role in helping to take care of him. Have you ANY IDEA what that period was like for me? I could not process what was happening. I was, and still am, absolutely devastated, confounded and out of my mind with grief and pain over Jonathan's death. You have lost your son. I have lost my husband, my friend, and the father of my children. To not accurately reflect my role during that period is, as I said in my earlier email, disrespectful and hurtful. Drawing attention to this is not acting out a 'self-obsessed fantasy.' It is what you call telling the truth.*

5. *And now, finally, you are blaming me for not knowing about the memorial service on the 14th February. This was organised by David and Jonathan's colleagues – NOT ME. The only funeral I organised I informed you about it and gave you updates – the response from you was to turn around and criticise me for 'allowing Jonathan's decomposing body to be viewed in church.' When David informed me about the service I assumed he had informed Tom too – like he had informed everyone else. Is it really my job, when trying to deal with the depressing and deeply sad milestone of Jonathan's first birthday since his death, to run around and make sure [that] you and the whole world know about the arrangement to which I was not part of organising when that is the job of the organiser? Are you serious? And even then I see that David did inform you of it, albeit the day before. Is it my fault too that you were not able to make last minute arrangements to attend? ... Keeping you informed of all*

developments, especially when it was the job of others to do so, when I am in deep mourning, was not, I am afraid, my first priority.

Patricia, I am tired. Do you know that since Jonathan's death I have been overwhelmed by the kindness of so many people. Most of whom were virtual strangers before Jonathan's death. The only exception to that has been you, Tom and June. You in particular have exhausted me with your accusations, your nitpicking, your sense of entitlement, your judgement and the way that you have consistently hurt me and then expected me to just 'get over it' by professing love and affection but with no genuine apology or remorse for your actions. If nothing else comes out of these email exchanges perhaps now you will begin to understand that you CANNOT treat people in this way and expect them to carry on as normal. The hurt is too raw and too deep for that.

You say you are 'finished and done' with making approaches to me in your email below. Well. If that is the price that I have to pay for peace and the space and time that I need to try and get through the worst period of my life and get my sons through this distressing period – then so be it. Thelma'

I felt utter relief when the email was sent. I was so tired of her. I wanted her and her family out of my head where they had appeared to take up permanent residence. I wanted to be free of them. So my heart thumped when a few hours later I saw another email from Rebecca pop up. *What now?!:*

The missile I expected from Patricia never materialised. Instead, when I gingerly crept out from my bunker and looked at the email I saw that it was from Tom sent via my lawyer. My surprise soon gave way to something else as I read the brief three line exchange from him. He wanted to put on record that all emails and letters that he had sent to me had come directly from him – and were not 'influenced' in any way by his mother. Then he added curtly with *'We agree that all exchanges must stop.'* That was it.

I felt deep disappointment when I read the email. I had initially imagined that Tom's intervention was to try and resolve things, to bang heads together and sort things out. But no – it was to put an end to all communications. The way that he was so quick to end all ties, to walk away really upset me. I felt a distinct lack of compassion and care from Jonathan's brother. Patricia was a nightmare but at least she showed some interest in her grandchildren. By contrast, Tom, in concert with his wife, was cold – particularly to his dead brother's children.

It disturbed me. And appalled me.

Not just for my sake but for those of my sons. How unlucky they were to lose their father and to be exposed to a distant and uninterested uncle. Their lives had changed so drastically since Jonathan's death – their whole world, their family had overnight become confined to just a few people in their lives. And now, with this severing of ties, especially where it appeared to be endorsed and wholeheartedly supported by Tom (with a ruthlessness that still took my breath away), it had narrowed even further.

My poor boys.

It took a while to shake myself out of the trough of despair and depression generated by the latest communications with the family. However, as time went on I tried to pick up the threads of my life. My routine became settled, filled with work four times a week and then the Fridays which I would have off, finding that it was not quite enough downtime for me before having full care of the boys by myself at the weekend and then having to go back to work on Monday. As challenging as it was though, I threw myself into the work, into my new identity. I did enjoy being back in the thick of work, but my mental health started to suffer. I felt ever so slightly the tight ball inside me starting to unravel.

I had had it in mind to get round to finding a bereavement counsellor for myself – as I had found for Dominic, but this had not been my first priority given the number of tasks I needed to undertake after Jonathan's death and starting a new job. I began to realise that this should be moved to the top of my agenda so I found a local therapist who had a slot available on Fridays – fast becoming the day I would use to schedule all of the life admin appointments and tasks that I could no longer undertake during the rest of the week. I started having sessions with her and thought that this could be the way to unpick the events of the last few months and to eventually start to properly process my grief. I finally began to think that I may have a pathway to a new life – a job, a counsellor, and my boys and that these need be the only things to focus on in the immediate future.

Again, as is always the case with me, I was wrong.

Very wrong.

I was about to be thrown a new challenge, one that would change the shape of things to come: the Covid pandemic and lockdown.

CHAPTER 10

The Widow

I am sure that I am not the only one whose life got turned upside down by the pandemic and by the lockdown that followed. From my part, there was absolutely no inkling that the background news about the SARS-like virus which was starting to spread in China would have any relevance to my life back in London. And so, like a lot of people, this news was digested and then promptly ignored. As the cases rose and it became apparent that it had spread into Europe again this did not feature highly on my radar.

It was now early March 2020. The beginning of spring. And four and a half months since Jonathan had died. I was at that point completely ensconced in work, in looking after my boys and in keeping my grief at bay – these all took up my entire energy and focus – I had time for little else.

By the time it became apparent that this was going to have some impact in our lives, when the fear of Covid became more pronounced, I welcomed the energy that this new virus brought into our lives. It was a talking point, a distraction and a means to bond with new work colleagues. I remember sitting in the work cafeteria talking to one of the mentors who had been assigned to me and we spent the session primarily talking about Italy and how over the top it seemed for the Italians to bring their whole country to a standstill with a lockdown. That kind of madness would never happen here in the UK – perish the thought!

However, with each day that went by, with its constant domination of the daily news cycle, a low level fear began to grip. In some ways it was reminiscent of what it must feel like at the beginning of an apocalypse – denial and fear vying for space in your brain with denial largely winning out, at least at the beginning.

The rumours began to abound that the UK may be headed for the same lockdown. Again, without first-hand knowledge of what that would mean in practice the idea of it did not strike fear in my heart. In fact, the first stage of restrictions I actually embraced. I had been working for about two months at the firm and even though my joy at finding a job and a purpose had not diminished, I was finding that I was becoming extraordinarily tired. Mentally and emotionally I felt robotic and largely unfocused, and physically, the daily commute, the long hours of work, the full-on childcare responsibilities which I had to navigate by myself, especially at the weekends – all of it was beginning to take its toll. About six weeks after starting work I came down with an infection, my immune system clearly under a lot of pressure from all the stress I was enduring. This added to my exhaustion and my struggle to keep going physically. When one of my son's had a birthday party to attend, one of the other parents had offered to help look after my other son. I grabbed at this help with relief and practically ran home so that I could get some sleep before I had to do the inevitable pick up. I was not coping well but I did not stop to rethink the situation and the amount of responsibilities I had on my plate.

I was on the tube going home when the news broke that new restrictions would be in place with almost immediate affect – all those who could work from home must work from home. I am ashamed to say that when this was announced,

I did not mind this at all. I felt very comfortable with this situation. There would be no more morning rush or commute. I could work in my home environment whilst the kids were at school and then when they returned, I could decamp upstairs from the living room and continue working for the day whilst my new nanny took over and looked after them. This dream scenario lasted no more than a week – before I read the headlines about Wales and Scotland deciding to shut their schools. That was when I began to feel a deep uneasiness. What if England followed suit – what then? I did not need to wait long to find out the answer to that – after one glorious week of working from home with the children in school, that was now to end: all schools in England would now be shut.

I could not believe it.

In that moment I could feel the house of cards that I had built up come crashing down. I knew then and there that it would be an unmitigated nightmare for me – it would be hell. My assessment of the situation was shared by some parent mums at the time.

Shortly after the announcement, whilst at the school gate collecting my boys on what would be one of the last occasions before schools shut, I encountered one of the other mums there. She was not one of those that I was especially close to but we were on speaking terms. She gave me a look that conveyed a mixture of pity and deep discomfort almost bordering on disgust (or so it seemed to me) and noted how difficult things would be for me now that schools were shut, saying poignantly, 'first the death of Jonathan and now this.' I did not how to respond to that. I should have prepared myself however, because as I soon discovered, she would not be the only one to give me that same look of pity and discomfort. Whilst shopping in the local supermarket later that same day

I bumped into another mother who clearly felt uncomfortable speaking to me about it, especially when I mentioned that Richard's 4th birthday was coming up. She responded quickly, 'Oh well, we will have to have lots of Zoom parties!' before making her excuses and hurriedly leaving with her shopping. I had no idea that such a thing as 'Zoom parties' even existed but her reaction towards me was clear – I made people feel very wary. Those parents who recognised how difficult things would be for me simply could not look me in the eye, because they saw in me the epitome of all that could go wrong in such a short time – and no doubt they did not want that reminder lest it be contagious and affect their own lives. In another time and place I may well have understood that – that kind of reaction being very similar to what some of us do when we pass homeless people on the street or those that have fallen on serious hard times and have been pummelled by life's knock-backs – we avert our eyes, we keep moving, distancing ourselves from the disaster, protecting ourselves and our loved ones because ultimately everyone looks after their own and we do not wish to be tarnished with the same brush. The only problem was that this was happening to *me*. I did not want to be the object of pity and revulsion because of circumstances beyond my control.

And yet I was.

It felt deeply hurtful and isolating. It made me feel worthless. However, I had to carry on – if not for my sake, then for the sake of my two sons. And the first port of call was in trying to understand and navigate this awful situation where my primary school aged children would be at home with me.

Every day.

And I would be expected to homeschool them.

Every day.
Whilst maintaining a full-time new job.
A job for which I was still on probation.
And I would be expected to do this all on my own.
Every day.
My initial attempts to call out this situation for the unfairness and absurdity of it all was met with resistance. Whilst walking with my sons to school for the last time before it closed, I bumped into another mother walking with her son. Gloria had been so helpful to me at times, her son and mine having recently taken up tennis at her urging. She had been very sympathetic after the death of my husband. So as I launched into a negative and vitriolic attack on the situation concerning the closure of schools and the fact that we would all be expected to homeschool children whilst working, her response was muted and defiantly positive, 'I'm sure it will all be fine. We will all manage somehow!' Will we? *Really?*

How on earth were 'we' supposed to do that? Perhaps I felt the panic and fear of the situation more keenly than others because part and parcel of my new found widowhood was that I was all alone now – with no husband and no partner.

I had no one.

This lockdown and all it would mean ensured that I would now be tested severely as a single parent.

And I had no doubt that I would be found wanting.

I would be found out.

I would fail.

Gloria's reaction highlighted just how alone I was in thinking from the outset that this whole situation would be an absolute disaster. This was echoed in one of the last text messages I received from Kathy right at the beginning of the school closure. Up until now I had seen her as one my anchors helping me so much during this period. However, it was clear that this lockdown had prompted in her a distancing from me. I simply could not escape the feeling that I was viewed as some sort of burden because as supportive and caring as her texts were, it was clear that she wanted to extricate herself from the responsibility of having to continually be there for me. Just as importantly however, she clearly did not share my views on what I thought the lockdown would be like – ignoring the part of my text where I referred to the situation as a 'dystopian nightmare'. It hurt, but the pride in me rose to the surface – again I did not want pity or to be viewed as some sort of problem child. I resolved then that I would not call out for help. I would deal with this, as I have dealt with nearly every challenging thing in my life so far: I would deal with it on my own.

Even so, my decision not to reach out for help could not include the workplace – on this they surely had to see that this was an impossible situation? I sent an email to the HR department naively setting out the fact that I was on my own, I had two young children whom I was expecting to homeschool whilst also working from home. I asked if the firm would be able to organise childcare for my boys so I could work (!). The response was polite but unhelpful – the main headline being: lockdown childcare is not available here – but thank you for reaching out. Undeterred, I spoke to a member of the HR team on the phone:

'I am on my own – my husband is not here. I have got two young children aged three and seven and I have to homeschool them. I am struggling to see how I can do a full day's work when I have sole care of my kids.'

'The firm understands that this is a challenging time for everyone. The official position is that everyone should just do the best they can.' The HR lady sounded very nice. But firm.

I paused, confused. 'I don't mean to press but what does that mean? What if my "best" is very little? What then?'

'As I said, the firm just wants everyone to do the best they can. We are all in the same position.'

I doubt that very much, I thought as we finished our conversation. I was left none the wiser.

Bollocks.

ॐ   ॐ   ॐ

I can say this with a great deal of conviction and I know that I am certainly not alone in feeling this – but I absolutely *hated* the lockdown. *Hated it.* I felt trapped as though stuck in a cage, completely stripped of all the resources and structures I had set up to try and support myself and the boys following Jonathan's death. I was now stuck at home, by myself, with two young boys, largely indoors, having to look after them whilst also trying to work. And whilst cut off from all other physical human contact.

Hell indeed.

The closure of schools coincided with the beginning of the Easter school holidays. This turned out to be quite fortuitous as I had already booked 'leave' from work so that I did not have to work for much of the time that the boys were on holiday. It also turned out to be a blessing in disguise because the infection that I had caught several weeks ago had not, despite a course of antibiotics, left me. In fact the infection had gotten worse so that by the time my boys were at home with me permanently, I was quite ill. By now the fear of Covid had taken hold and I became scared the more ill I became. There was no way to know for sure because widespread testing was not available then but I became convinced that I must have Covid. I coughed up phlegm forcefully, my body exhausted from the strength needed to complete each coughing fit. My chest felt completely constricted and in those moments when I struggled to breathe I feared for my life and the life of my boys. With no one allowed to be in the house with me and no one able to help I still had to continue looking after the boys – feeding them, bathing them, looking after them even as I was doubled over with weakness and tiredness. One night, after struggling to breathe I called 111, scared and alone, wondering if this was it – even as the computerised voice took me through the lengthy and largely irrelevant questionnaire. The result was that I was to await a call back. I then tried to sleep but I could not. I was genuinely scared that if I drifted off I would not wake again. That was a scary night. I eventually did fall asleep, and the next day still woke up ill but feeling a touch better. The nurse who rang me prescribed another course of antibiotics. Gradually, I began to recover. As I did, and before the holiday and my sick leave expired, I turned my mind to the subject of what I was going to do about work and homeschooling. I felt the support that I had from the parent mums had drained away completely. There were some exceptions of course – Gloria offering to grab some items for me when she went to the local shop and Lucy ringing me from time to time to check on me – but ultimately everyone became more inward looking, focusing on their own lives and on their families.

I felt so alone.

But I still had a job to do.

I was genuinely perplexed by my situation. How on earth could I work and simultaneously look after a three year old and a seven year old on my own? I did some research on what people could actually do during the lockdown. There seemed to be conflicting advice but legally I could not find anything which would stop nannies doing their job – and of course they would still need to work. And so after communicating with May (a local nanny who lived very close by) and Rachel (the nanny who had taken over from Valerie), I agreed a rota with them – they would look after the boys full time, take them through their homeschooling and effectively provide the childcare whilst I stayed at my desk and worked. This turned out to be the best solution. I am well aware that this was not in keeping with the spirit of the lockdown but I felt I had no choice – there was no other way to square the circle. If I was to work, I needed childcare – and to afford childcare I needed to work. The two nannies formed a bubble with our three families and this became an effective way for us all to function.

For the boys I am sure that it helped them enormously to not be entirely cut off from the world. In Richard's case, despite everything, he had retained his innate cheeriness and optimism over the last few months. However, after schools and nurseries shut and he was confined indoors day after day, he began to change quite noticeably – transforming into a boy suffering from depression – being quiet and withdrawn for a lot of the time – not wanting to engage much with either me or his brother. The most frightening thing for me during that period was when he looked so sad and solemn. This occurred with increasing frequency as time wore on and it made me feel helpless. It was a relief then and very good for him and for Dominic that they were looked after by two hardworking nannies who nurtured them and cared for their needs whilst I worked, especially May, who lived nearby. She made a point of taking them out quite a bit and the interactions with her and her own two children meant that the boys at least were mixing with their peers and had playmates. This allowed me the time to focus on my work.

And focus I did.

The amount of time I spent at my desk, looking at a computer, going from one Zoom meeting to another cannot be described. I certainly tried my best, even if I sometimes felt overwhelmed by it all, and a bit out my depth – but I ploughed on. I enjoyed my work for the large part but I also became very slowly stir crazy. It was almost the case of having too much of a good thing – I certainly had my wish to take a break from the daily commute into work. However, I did not ever think that being at the desk for such long periods of time would result in me pining for the opportunity to throw on a suit and venture out just so I could interact with others and feel part of the world again.

I worked very long hours. Soon it was not unusual for me to stop at about 6 pm when the boys would return home, sort out their dinner and their baths, put them to bed and then log on again in the evening at around 9 pm to keep on working. I sometimes worked even at the weekends. There was one occasion when the boys were away for the whole day on Saturday and instead of resting, I used the time to piece together a presentation on a new area of law which I was giving to clients along with my colleagues. This was very exhilarating but also extremely challenging. I had very little downtime for myself and rarely had a chance to take any lengthy breaks, not even on a Friday, my day off.

I was going slowly insane from all the hours of work and the sitting at my desk so I started trying to incorporate some exercise into my daily lunchtimes. At first this was using the bouncer that I had bought just for that purpose, but I began to get tetchy from being indoors for such long stretches of time. I started going outside and took up running again as the weather got better. It was a slow process but I stuck to it and managed to include that into my routine.

In the end, my work regime was clearly successful because at the end of my probation period I was offered a full-time position as a lawyer and was kept on by the law firm in the early summer of 2020. At about the same time, I was selected to feature in an article in a newsletter circulated by the agency that placed me, about successful lawyers who had managed to reignite their legal career after taking a career break. Career wise, against all the odds I was a success.

So why did I feel so empty inside?

Even as it was announced and I thanked the senior partners for the opportunity they were giving me, I felt detached and disconnected. It suddenly did not seem right. The enthusiasm that I once had when I started the job, the joy that I had striding to work all those months ago had faded. I was now left with the reality of the situation – I would be wedded to my desk, working remotely, attending Zoom meeting after Zoom meeting and forever trying to balance my work with the needs of my children. I suddenly found the whole prospect very, *very* daunting. The gnawing doubts about work I kept at bay however – I could not deal with it just yet.

As we moved further into the summer I welcomed the changes to the boys' routine. Richard's nursery contacted me stating that they could offer Richard a place at nursery and he could form part of a bubble with other vulnerable children who needed to go back into a school environment. This was a great opportunity for Richard and it was good for him to go back to some form of nursery setting before he would begin reception at school. This left Dominic. With Richard back at nursery it became obvious that he became disjointed and was a bit lonely. I decided to write to his school and request that he be able to attend. With some relief, my request was quickly granted and he was able to attend school as a vulnerable child. It made a huge difference to the boys to go back to some form of formal structure and routine – something which had been badly missing since the lockdown. That normality also made it easier for them when the summer holiday started. This was because we would soon have to deal with another first – the first family holiday without Jonathan.

   ℣ ℣ ℣

During the dark days of the Christmas period, on impulse, I had booked a holiday for me and the boys in the summer – more as a way to cheer us up than anything else. When the lockdown ensued it was not clear whether we (or anyone else) would be able to go on holiday at all. However, as the lockdown restrictions began to ease in the lead up to summer, it became apparent that some holidays would be allowed.

 When Jonathan was alive our family holidays had gravitated towards what Jonathan wanted (and what our budget allowed) which was a family holiday in the South of France, staying in a gite and of course self-catering. As authentic as those holidays were, with two young children, this was actually quite a lot of work for me. There was still cooking, washing, cleaning and other domestic chores to be done. So when booking the holiday to Greece, I decided to go for a very different type of holiday. One that would be as far removed as possible from the type of holidays we would normally have. I booked a holiday with an organisation that specifically catered for single people going away with their children, thinking that booking with such a company would make it less lonely for the boys and I. I also purposefully (and perversely) wanted a holiday that was as different in nature as it could possibly be to the kind of quiet thoughtful adventures that Jonathan had preferred. So the resort in Crete where we ended up was a very large one with many families, swimming pools, kids activity clubs, night entertainment and many, *many* restaurants and cafes with large selections of food at the buffet. It was as loud as our gite in the South of France was quiet, with music blaring from loud speakers as we wound our way from one end of the resort to another.

I liked it.

I liked the fact that for the first time on holiday I did not have to worry about cooking and cleaning. Nor did I have to worry about the entertainment. I could just relax and do *nothing*. But most important of all, what I feared the most, was that the boys and I were not alone. At all times we were surrounded by many other families and by a resort that was a buzzing hive of constant activity. At that moment that was what we needed.

Even so, there were times in my interactions with others that there seemed to be a lack of understanding about our situation – that we were a grieving family. I remember one lady with her daughters who was on holiday as part of the single parents group package. She listened as I told her about Jonathan's death, the suddenness of it and the fact that the boys and I were still dealing with this loss. She immediately compared it to her messy divorce and the loss that that had generated. I felt in that moment like screaming at her and saying, 'No, it is not the same. You lost a husband but your children still *have* a father. My children have lost their father. *Forever!*'

I said nothing.

I smiled politely and turned away, completely numbed by the conversation. Despite this, as a whole, the summer holiday was a very welcome distraction from our lives, before we returned back home to reality with a bump.

As autumn descended I found myself struggling more and more with work. It was not just that I could not find the enthusiasm for it any longer, I was simply not in the right frame of mind mentally. I now found the prospect of working in the long term whilst my head remained a fog of unresolved feelings and grief terrifying. I would sneak off during my lunchtime to nap after my run just so I could escape and have peace from the demands of deadlines and having to always be on top of things – something which I felt I patently was not. The burden of work became heavier and heavier and began to dominate my therapy sessions. In my sessions during that period I spoke incessantly about how I had begun to have doubts about work and yet the prospect of leaving made me feel so guilty. I felt constantly that whatever I did I would be letting people down – my work colleagues and mentors and those who had hired me if I quit. But if I did not quit I didn't think I could successfully keep juggling all the balls in the air of work, the boys and homelife. The same questions kept going round in my head: What if I screwed up? Made a horrifying mistake? What then?

I felt paralysed by fear unable to move in either direction.

I have no doubt that one of the other things playing in the background was that I would soon be approaching another 'first' since Jonathan's death. This first was the big one: the most significant one of all – the actual anniversary of Jonathan's death. Even though objectively I felt that I was ready for this, subconsciously I am not clear that I was. One of the reasons this was on my mind in a big way was that shortly after we returned from holiday, I had a surprise email waiting for me in my inbox.

It was from Patricia.

The email sent to me via my lawyer was shorter than I was used to from Patricia, a mere three or so paragraphs this time. It began by asking after me and the boys whilst also providing an update on how she and Vincent had fared during the lockdown (with gardening featuring very heavily). She asked about appropriate gifts for the boys and invited me to give her suggestions as she was keen to send them something soon to mark their return to school in a couple of weeks. The email ended with a few photos of her garden, a couple of which included Vincent – looking worn and old but with a smile on his face.

My first reaction upon receiving the email was almost a form of panic. The ball of dread, my constant companion from the past swept in, taking up residence again in my stomach. I could feel the outer edges of a headache beginning to form. With the exception of a brief exchange of emails over the Easter period via my lawyer concerning Richard's birthday gifts there had been no correspondence with the family for months. And I had relished the silence. It had given me the space to breathe. I had just begun to think that perhaps I would be free of having much to do with them. But no, it was not to be. Here was Patricia, sending me another email, enticing me back into her world. I read the email carefully. I paused when I saw the photo of Vincent again, looking at it carefully this time. The photo was of my father-in-law but all I saw when I stared at the photo in that instant was Jonathan. The eyes, the smile, even the expression – it was Jonathan again. I took a deep breath and collected myself. *Not now. Not now.* I went back to the email.

On the face of it, it seemed pleasant enough with a complete erasing of all the acrimony of the past. It was confusing and I did not know what to make of it. My first instinct was to continue the wall of silence and ignore it. I had enough on my plate to be dealing with – I did not need any more drama from Patricia and her gang. On the other hand, putting aside my pride, would that be the right decision to make, especially taking into account my boys and what they needed? Would they want to be estranged from their father's side of the family forever, particularly their father's mother with whom they had established a bond before Jonathan had died? Especially as Patricia did seem to care for the boys in her own way. On that issue I could not fault her. As uncomfortable as it made me, and with a great deal of reluctance, I decided to respond honestly to Patricia about my position and how I felt:

'*[Patricia], I have seen your email to me below. After a lot of thought I have decided to respond to you directly.*

A famous person once started a letter to another person by apologising first for the length of it, because he did not have the time to make the letter shorter. I am sure you know who that person was (I'm afraid that I cannot recall who it was). Well I am in a similar position now. This is a long email. You will need to bear with it.

I have told you this story before, about the honeymoon that Jonathan and I took in Nepal. It is clear to me that you forgot this story throughout the time that Jonathan was ill and died – your behaviour to me and that of your family is proof of this. Let me remind you of this story again.

Jonathan and I started our honeymoon in Nepal the day after our wedding. Everything was good at first. The scenery was absolutely amazing and the whole trip was exciting. The only negative thing to begin with was the pollution in Kathmandu – absolutely appalling. But no matter we thought – we were only there for a day or so before we started our trek.

Once we started our trek we were amazed by the stunning scenery. I was very glad I came. Jonathan had been completely responsible for organising the trip to Nepal whilst I had concentrated on organising the wedding so he received a lot of credit for the trip.

However, as we went further on in the Annapurna Trek and climbed higher and higher Jonathan began to feel unwell. At first we thought it was just food poisoning, which was plausible given the exotic new dishes that we were exposed to. But Jonathan did not improve. By the time we reached a major camp, a mere day or so before we reached the peak, Jonathan became incapacitated and was bedridden.

As a doctor, Jonathan of course tried to diagnose himself. He thought it was food poisoning combined with some other infection. He touched upon mountain sickness but did not really entertain the possibility that he had it as he had other symptoms which were more consistent with food poisoning. In any event, he could not move and we could not carry on. I was deeply worried. I asked our guide about turning back. The guide was not keen on this, saying he was sure that Jonathan would get better after a day or so of rest and we could carry on but I was not sure about this.

This camp we were at was the epicentre for a climbing organisation that funded treks and climbs in the areas. As such they were hosting an event for trekkers and climbers – giving them advice, equipment, resources etc. ... They were also giving a presentation that day. I decided to attend and told the guide to take me. Again he was not terribly keen but I insisted. I told Jonathan that I was going round the corner for this talk in the hope of getting some advice for his condition. Jonathan of course decided that he would like me to ask the people there a few questions and made me memorise 2 or 3 questions to ask – that was it – he was insistent that he did not need anything else! Well, I thought, I will ask the questions but I will also try and buy some medication if I could because Jonathan was really ill.

As I listened to this talk, which was on mountain sickness I began to get even more worried. The symptoms of mountain sickness were absolutely consistent with Jonathan's symptoms. In fact I recall a slide with a symptom checker that had about 5 symptoms listed – Jonathan's symptoms ticked nearly all of them. I was quite alarmed now.

After the talk I spoke to one of the doctors about Jonathan. I remember the guide again tried to dissuade me but at this stage I was just ignoring his advice. I approached the doctor, a very nice young female doctor and spoke to her about Jonathan. I asked if she could come back to the hotel we were in and see Jonathan. By now, the 2–3 questions that Jonathan wanted [me] to ask had completely gone out of my head. She told me she could come back but there would be a fee. I paid with my credit card and we all walked back. I thought Jonathan may be cross that I had not followed his instructions (in fact I knew he would definitely be cross) but I decided that it was a risk I would have to take. I felt much more comfortable having a medical professional who could properly assess him.

And she did and the diagnosis was prompt – acute mountain sickness. Jonathan needed to go down to ground level. Immediately. She arranged for us to have a helicopter to take us back down to Kathmandu and we left by the end of the day. As soon as we got off the mountain and was back at ground level Jonathan recovered – literally overnight he was well again. Had he stayed up there for a few more days he would have died.

When Jonathan was at Charing Cross Hospital I teased him about this. I said to him, 'Do you remember Nepal?' and even though he was so weak and so ill he smiled and said 'yes, you saved my life.'

When I saw him deteriorating before my very eyes I wanted him in hospital. I wanted him to get better. I wanted to save his life again. Because the last time that Jonathan had been a doctor and patient at the same time I had had to override him and make a decision about his welfare and I had got it right that time. I thought I could do the same.

[Patricia], I do not and probably will not ever forgive you for the way you and your family have treated me. I have made my feelings clear on the subject and I won't repeat them now suffice to say that you got me completely and utterly wrong. And if it was not for my two sons I doubt that I would remain in contact following your family's treatment of me over the last year. But for Dominic and Richard's sake I must consider what is best for them.

My boys, especially Dominic, miss you (and Vincent). This is not surprising. You formed a bond with the boys when Jonathan as alive and you have maintained a level of contact with them since his death. Dominic speaks about his 'grandma in the countryside'. Not always, but often enough for me to know you are in his thoughts. I know he would want to maintain contact with you. It would help with his grief and that of Richard too. And the two boys have been dealing with so much grief. Along with the pandemic they have had to cope *with an enormous amount of upheaval and with only me to help them and guide them. That's right [Patricia] – I have had to cope too with an extraordinary amount – dealing with my grief, the boys' grief, homeschooling them through a pandemic and all whilst trying to carry on with my new job. My mother, the only family member who could offer any substantial help has been extremely unwell during this period and could not help (and even if she could she would be shielding so any help would have been extremely limited). That of course leaves you and Jonathan's side of the family. Your family's lack of support, criticism and judgment has been detrimental not just to me but to Dominic and Richard – denying them family members who purport to love Jonathan but (with the exception of you who at least has shown some consideration for the boys since his death) have decided quite easily in a cold and callous manner to turn their backs on his flesh and blood, his pride and joy, his two sons. Words leave me at this point. I still find this deeply shocking and distressful for my sons.*

Let me be clear again Patricia. You have not apologised for the way you have treated me but even if you did I must be honest and say that I would struggle to forgive you and your family. But I would be a hypocrite if I accused you of putting your own needs first above that of your grandsons if I do the same and ignore their needs too because I am too angry and embittered with you and your family. I do not want that on my conscience.

So for their sake I am willing to engage with you so they can connect with someone in their father's family who actually cares for them and who they care for too.

So to answer your questions – you are welcome to send the boys gifts. Dominic would be happy with any gift including the watch that you mentioned. What would be helpful however is a gift linked to music and especially to the violin. During the lockdown I applied for him to obtain a music scholarship after his music teacher encouraged me to do so. His application was successful and he will start his scholarship lessons with the violin from this September with the aim of joining a London orchestra. His love of music clearly comes from Jonathan and a gift linked to this would mean an awful lot to him. As for Richard, he is at the beginning of his grief journey and with each day comes the realisation that his father is gone. What would help him are any toys (or similar toys) which Jonathan had at Richard's age. It would help to connect him to his father at this time. Also any gifts linked to him starting school. He is very proud of the fact that he is now 'a big boy' who will be starting school next term after 'graduating' from nursery earlier this year.

In the interim I have shown the boys the recent photo of [Vincent] that you sent. I think they would welcome a recent photo of you too – Dominic especially would like that very much.

It is likely that Dominic will write soon and send you a postcard from our recent holiday – so watch out for that in the next week or so.

I will let the boys know you will soon be in contact with them again.

Until then, Thelma.'

The response from Patricia was immediate and surprising. She expressed her gratitude for my actions in Nepal – she and Tom had agreed that without my intervention Jonathan would likely have died. She also set out in detail (in a paragraph devoted solely to this purpose) how Jonathan's life had turned out for the better after meeting me and having Dominic and

Richard, despite the difficult times I had endured both before and after giving birth to them. She was warm and effusive in her praise of me. I found this jarring in many ways being a complete contrast to what I had experienced with her over the past year.

But the real surprise was in the next paragraph. It was not just the fulsome apology which I received that astonished me (*'I apologise unreservedly for any distress I caused you by what I said or did or what I did not say or do to help you ...'*). It was the frank acknowledgement she made about my role during Jonathan's illness and death. She now realised that I had *'bore the brunt'* of Jonathan's illness, that I had been with him day and night, caring for him in hospital, responsible for arranging the funeral service by myself all whilst having sole responsibility and care for my two children. In doing all this I was *'the strongest of us all.'* She then rounds the email off by congratulating me on my new job, expressing admiration for Dominic's musical skills and sending her love to us all.

Well, well.

I sat back in my chair and let my mind go blank. There was too much emotion to decipher – I needed to just be numb. Just for a few moments.

She had apologised, which must have been a big step for her in many ways. I pondered that for a long while. As I did, the numbness began to shift and then all of a sudden, like a dam that had been filled to capacity and which had now broken, I felt my rage and anger towards her ebb away forcefully and uncontrollably. It suddenly seemed so pointless to continue with the vendetta. I was tired of it.

I have no doubt that Jonathan would not have wanted us to continue arguing. For my boys' sake and for my sanity it seemed better to go with the flow and to accept this olive branch being offered.

I took my time to craft my response to her:

'Dear [Patricia],

Thank you for your email. I appreciate your candour and your kind words.

I agree with you that grief is extremely complex. Particularly in this case with Jonathan where his death was so quick and abrupt and was so wholly unexpected (at least at this stage in our lives – yes I know we all die eventually but Jonathan was healthy and fit – I did not expect to be a widow for many, many years to come). But as you say life goes on. And for those like us with dependents it must go on – there is no choice. In that vein I agree we should now move forward in the way Jonathan would like us to.

So concerning [Dominic's] musical gift you can leave that for now and concentrate on buying him the watch. We have only just had our first meeting with the scholarship team. [Dominic] will start his solo lessons and lessons with the orchestra in the next few weeks. I will wait and see what his music teacher says about any materials he may need – and if it is not covered by the scholarship then I will let you know. That would be most useful to [Dominic] and can form part of any birthday gift or Christmas gift later in the year.

By now (I hope) you should have received the postcard that [Dominic] wrote and sent to you. In the absence of seeing you both in person, the boys ([Dominic] especially), is now keen to have a Zoom session with you and Vincent. I do not know how you feel about this – let me know if you are fine with this (or simple FaceTime on WhatsApp) and I will let the boys know and help to set it up.

I will wait to hear from you,
Until then,
Thelma.'

And with that the relations with Patricia were thawed sufficiently for the boys to have contact and access with their grandparents. The first Zoom session we set up was emotional. It was odd seeing them across the screen. The boys were so very happy to see them. I don't believe that tears were shed at the time but I felt the raw emotions of seeing Jonathan's parents again after almost a year. It felt like a real turning point for me in many ways.

Shortly after that was the anniversary of Jonathan's death. I decided the day itself would be too difficult for a visit to the grave. It would be too overwhelming for the boys. It would be too overwhelming for me. So on 25 October 2020, on the anniversary of Jonathan's death, I took the boys on a fun day out instead. We went to visit the London Aquarium and we had an amazing day looking at the fish and all the other aquatic forms of life. The next day we then visited the grave and although it may have seemed strange to do it in this order it felt right. Standing by the graveside with just Dominic and Richard, I felt fully now that it was just us three against the world. We were on our own and we had to forge our lives forward in a way that was true to ourselves, but would also be true to Jonathan.

The feeling of needing to be true to ourselves stayed with me for days afterwards. And it became the catalyst for me to make the huge decision that I had been battling with for months. On that day in late October, as I was running on the street, completing a loop before heading for home, I fell over on the pavement. I collapsed on the ground in a heap with torn clothes and a badly bloodied and bruised knee and fought back tears. I felt in that moment my vulnerability and fear. It was clear to me, as I hobbled back to my home, unable to walk properly let alone run, that my trying to carry on was futile. I was injured, I could not run for now. I was also emotionally and mentally injured, I should not be carrying on as though I was OK.

And I no longer wanted to.

A few days later I went to my GP and was effectively signed off sick – anxiety and grief-related depression. By now I had told my workplace the full situation of my being widowed. They were incredibly understanding – which was contrary to the fears of retribution that I had entertained at the prospect of letting them down. I had no idea what the future held or whether I could honestly ever return to work but I knew that I had to be honest with myself about my grief, which was now coming to the surface in spades. Being signed off sick for an indefinite period gave me the space that I needed to start the journey of beginning to process the loss that I had been keeping at bay for so many months. It also meant that I could stand still and be there for my boys as they needed me now more than ever. I would also need to process and make sense of my life with Jonathan as imperfect as it was, and our relationship which clearly had been troubled with the spectre of potential infidelities in the background, arguments and huge conflicts – I would need to decide how I felt about that, how this would affect my memory of him and how I viewed him in the future.

But.

He would always be my husband regardless and the father of my children.

And that was what mattered.

As I survey the detritus of my family life, the ruptures within the family structure on Jonathan's side of the family and the inability of those on my side of the family to be fully present and supportive of me in a coherent and consistent way, I realise that it all falls on me.

I will be alone as I navigate my grief.

I will be alone as I face the new world without Jonathan, with just me and the boys.

I will be alone as I accompany my sons as they undergo their own grief journey.

The burden I feel is overwhelming. It is immense. I am scared and I am broken. But the path I must walk is ahead now – I can no longer ignore it or bypass it or seek a short cut as I have done in the past. I must start the journey now. And I would begin that journey the only way I knew how – by standing still, breathing and then taking the first step.

THE END

TO BE CONTINUED
BOOK 2 COMING SOON